PRAISE FOR *MANIFEST YOUR*

Rebecca's Vision: A 'New Testament' of Love

Rebecca Skeele's magnificent new book is a gift to those of us who are seekers, those of us who are longing for more meaning in our lives and who quest in turn to manifest light into our world. Her words inspire us to delve deeply for inner wisdom and to trust the divine guidance and knowing which comes with connection to our higher selves. She gives us a practical roadmap to enable us to follow the process, to which she likens as an alchemical task of mining iron into gold.

The beauty of this process ultimately seeds co-creation, the germination of a new, blessed world. Her vision is clear, that in healing ourselves we heal the world. The bio-product of an expanded heart is the realization of our higher calling to live an inspired life.

I particularly appreciated Rebecca's emphasis on service. "Service is the highest form of loving," she writes with language so clear and illustrative. Her Christ-like wisdom of 'loving presence' resonates in each chapter and conveys the truth that becoming an enlightened , self-actualized person results in loving service to others. She refers to this vision as a 'New Testament' of love. Indeed, to love one another, we much first learn to love ourselves. This book brings us closer to a vision of beauty and hope for those of us who are seekers of our divine purpose, or our Sacred Ambition.

–The Rev. Dcn. Holly Galgano Deacon, Episcopal Church

A Soul Summons

Reading Manifest Your Sacred Ambition is like tuning into my soul, each page lovingly and compassionately beckoning me to step more fully into my essence. Rebecca's approach weaves inspiring divine wisdom with balanced real-world examples. It is refreshingly much more of an unveiling than a typical how-to. What I love most about this book is that the goodies keep coming – I can pick it back up, turn to any page, and find something that speaks to me in that moment. Fueling the sacred fire, Manifest Your Sacred Ambition is not only a book; it is a mission for these times.

– Shannon Brook Olson

Take Your Time and Give Yourself Space for Reading Rebecca's "Manifesto."

Reading and reviewing Rebecca Skeele's most recent book: Manifest Your Sacred Ambition has taken me longer than I had originally expected and for a good reason. Her bold calling and loving summons for "Heart's Work" not only offers but provides sacred space and time which must be savored, valued and reflected upon, deeply.

Rebecca is not only calling but continually reminding each of us to become engaged and live our lives with deeper significance, meaning and purpose. Like a measuring line stretched out in front and into the future as well as a memory string wound around one's index finger, MYSA serves both as guide and compass for Sacred Transformational Living.

Along the way many direct questions and helpful suggestions work to catalyze and recognize:

Calling: On Your Mark

Ambition: Get Set

Action: Go.

Do have a copy on your bedside table for reading at the beginning and/or end of the day and then you will clearly: hear your Call, recognize your Ambition and take your Action, with a deep soulful sacredness that will meaningfully benefit not only yourself, but others and the world.

– Prof. Jonathan Paul De Vierville PhD, MSSW, LCSW, LPC

Universal Truths About Humanity

In Rebecca Skeele's "Manifest Your Sacred Ambition" you will discover so much of yourself in each chapter you'll start to repeat "Hey! That's me!" Why? Because this book is about universal truths about humanity. In the "Sacred Calling" chapters Rebecca reveals what it means to be connected and truthful to your innermost calling ... the thing your heart wants you to do. In the second section, Sacred Ambition, Rebecca reveals the next steps in your evolution. It's about following your Sacred Calling and helping it enter your life in a real and substantial way. This means shedding fear. "Sacred Action," section three, is all about taking your calling and your ambition and bringing it into the world; unleashing the power of YOU that was always there but you hadn't realized.

After reading this I came to know so much more about me and my Sacred Nature."

– Aaron C. Yeagle

MANIFEST
YOUR
SACRED
AMBITION

Summon Your Heart's Calling
into Bold, Loving Action

Published by:

VINCA PUBLISHING LLC
3006 Governor Lindsey Rd.
Santa Fe, NM 87505

Vinca Publishing LLC
3006 Governor Lindsey Rd.
Santa Fe, NM 87505
www.vincapublishingllc.com

Published 2021

Editor: Jeff Braucher, Eve Tolpa
Book design and typography: Diane Rigoli
Cover design: Diane Rigoli
Author photo: Steve Cozart
© Copyright 2021 Rebecca E. Skeele

All rights reserved. No part of this publication may be repro-
duced in any form whatsoever without written permission from
the publisher, except for brief quotations embodied in literary
articles or reviews.

Printed in the United States of America

ISBN's:
978-0-9715674-7-4 (paperback)
978-0-9715674-9-8 (hardcover)
978-0-9715674-8-1 (e-book)

Library of Congress Control Number:
2021907721

I dedicate this book to you,
Beautiful Soul,
who holds a sacred calling in your heart.
Shine brightly!
We need you.

Contents

FOREWORD

SACRED AMBITION INVOLVES A DEEP, INNER CALLING TO each of us. This calling is grounded in compassion, love, and caring for the betterment of health and healing for all of humanity.

Reflect for a few moments on your calling. What are you hoping for? What are your desired outcomes? Next, reflect on our world. What do you think our current individual and collective challenges really involve? What do you imagine success will look and feel like when we recognize that we are one species united in a single, global village sharing a planetary destiny?

Sacred Ambition invites us to identify our soul's purpose. What is your life's meaning, intention, and focus? Without definite answers, we are not fully equipped to confront the challenges that are part of everyone's life.

This journey always involves healing. In the largest sense, healing is a lifelong journey toward wholeness. It involves opening to our innate ways of knowing that we have perhaps closed down in the face of life's constant difficulties and distractions. Our reawakening involves focusing on the strengths that we've forgotten, but which still exist, strengths that await a nudge to assert themselves once again — not just in service to ourselves but in service to others as well.

This path connects with our spirituality— our sense of connectedness with "something higher" — an absolute, immanent, or transcendent power, however named — and the conviction that meaning, value, direction and purpose are valid aspects of the universe.

When we grasp the universality of suffering, we realize there is plenty of it to go around. Suffering is truly universal, and the essence of compassion is a tenderness of the heart in response to suffering of *all* humans and *all* creatures. This is an invaluable recognition, because of our tendency to omit compassion toward ourselves.

Maya Angelou, the acclaimed author and poet, said, "There is no greater agony than bearing an untold story inside of you."[1] Everyone has their own story, so we cannot wait for others to tell *our* story. We must be the storyteller of our lives, even if we are the only one listening. What reflections are you sharing not only with others, but yourself? Do we realize that our personal story may strengthen others? What features of your story do you embrace and treasure? What aspects of your story make you *you*? What story will we leave? No one is storyless. Each of us is a unique, living narrative.

Living our story is often called "walking our talk." Our "talk" involves recognizing our sacred calling — growing into an expanded consciousness and a collective responsibility toward fostering healthy people living on a healthy planet. This is the evolved consciousness and evolutionary future toward which Sacred Ambition points.

At this moment on our imperiled planet, there has never been a greater need for a moral commitment to be global citizens — people with an expanded story, who recognized the intrinsic interconnectedness and unity among individuals, countries, and cultures, and who identify their belonging to a world community. This invariably involves strengthening our commitment to inclusion, diversity, equity, and justice.

In expanding our story, let us learn to celebrate the paradox of how individual responsibility and personal growth lead to unity, oneness and togetherness. On this recognition our future on this beautiful, generous planet depends.

– Barbara Dossey, PhD, RN
Author, *Florence Nightingale: Mystic, Visionary, Healer* and *Dossey and Keegan's Holistic Nursing: A Handbook for Practice*

---

[1] Maya Angelou. Quoted in: *Donna Cameron & Kristen Leathers. One Hill, Many Voices: Stories of Hope and Healing.* Centralia, WA: Gorham Printing; 2011: 190.

Sacred Calling: A Path of Self-Awakening and Self-Fulfillment

You Were Born for This Time

YOU WERE BORN TO BE THE ONE TO DO YOUR WORK, and no one else can do it like you can. You were born to reclaim your innate ambition and hold it as a sacred calling so you do not play small when the world needs you to be seen and heard. You were born to be empowered by your uniqueness, even your weirdness, and express the way your holiness wants to be expressed through you as you.

But many of us have felt, up until now, that what we had to offer the world was not valuable. Our gifts, talents, insights, visions, and dreams didn't seem to fit in anywhere. The world had a different agenda—an agenda of maintaining the status quo: Do it this way; look and talk like this; go to school, get an education and start your career; get married and have children (or devote all your energy to your career); retire and die.

But *your* timeline didn't unfold quite like that. Your life has had a different beat and taken you to places that were out of the norm.

And in following your own path, what you envisioned for this planet—for education, for a better way to do business, for co-creating change through shifting consciousness, for cooperative ideas about living together and sharing resources—often fell on deaf ears or, worse yet, were relegated to the fringe of society and not taken seriously.

The status quo traditions seemed to rule the day. Voices that shared something new or out of the ordinary—even extraordinary—were ignored and often silenced.

So perhaps you played small and hid behind the day-in-and-day-out routine of "Let me just get by and not rock the boat," or "I'll keep my head down and play along."

But while all this unfulfilling status quo has been relentlessly marching on, the seeds of that sacred calling, that haunting dream, that inspired creation, have not vanished. Even though you have kept these seeds out of sight and maybe even out of mind, the light of *who you are* has been preparing the day when the germination can no longer be impeded.

I am inviting you to say, "Today is that day. I will no longer minimize the fire in my belly and the love in my heart that is calling me forward to express and fulfill this sacred calling."

The Next Level

You have lived a courageous, purposeful life that mattered. And now it's time to step out, to take your life to its next level. Birthing your calling into the expanding space of your inner permission, releasing the fear and hesitation from the past, requires you to know who you are and what you are willing to commit, devote, and dedicate yourself to. This is where you must begin if you want your sacred calling to continue to take shape and form.

Sacred callings require you to stop settling, to wake up,
and to stand up within yourself for you.

Choosing Not to Settle Anymore

Laura had settled for the old story of staying in a job she could tolerate so she could retire with a nice 401(k). But at the same time, Laura knew her deeper calling: to bring more heart and soul into the corporate world. Her current corporate position was not making much of a dent.

She said to me, "I realized that my sacred calling was to empower executives to know and act from their deepest commitment as the CEO of their business so they could make their greatest contribution. And I needed to find those people outside the corporate world." So Laura left her lucrative corporate consulting business and began working with small-business owners who were making big changes in their culture through a noncompetitive, inclusive, and cooperative business model. They were redefining what success meant, and it included serving the greater good as well as the bottom line.

Sherri's path typifies another "old story": settling for what you are good at rather than taking a risk and embarking on a career that you are called into.

Sherri had put aside her sacred calling to make it as an advertising executive. But she always felt she had given up a lot. "Don't get me wrong," she said. "My years in advertising were good in many ways and allowed me to know that I had talent and ability, but it just wasn't enough." When she quit to get her master's in education, her life changed. "I found real purpose for the first time, and everything was easy! I came home to myself." Sherri's experience of "coming home" is a common response when we choose not to settle anymore—even if the money is good or the perks are fun or the status quo brings some joy. Quite honestly, the experience of "coming home" is priceless. And it can also be financially abundant, fun, and full of unexpected benefits.

Kim's story is also typical of what life looks like when we chase after those bright, shiny objects and ignore the call of the heart. Kim did not feel she fit in anywhere, so by the time she was in her late thirties or early forties she had bounced around from job to job, from start-up to start-up, not landing anyplace. The elephant in the room, Kim admits now, was the deeper journey of following the call of her heart and soul. But, wow, was that scary! "How am I going to make a living doing that?" Kim lamented. So the calling became more vocal and in her face.

Kim began receiving dreams that disturbed her. She felt oddly unsettled upon waking up and couldn't decide if the messages in the dreams were trying to tell her something was wrong or if they were literally trying to wake her up. She discovered it was both. "Yes, something was wrong in my life," she said. "I wasn't living my true calling. I had given it up because I was afraid: afraid of what people would think, my family, my friends. Afraid that I was fooling myself." Despite her fear, Kim began doing the inner work to free herself from unwanted and outdated limitations and allowed her inner guidance to show her the way. That is, she began following her sacred calling through listening to what was beckoning, and slowly the way began to emerge.

In these three typical scenarios, each courageous visionary had to grant herself the permission
to move beyond settling and consider the cost. And
for each one, the cost became unbearable.

They had to ask themselves: *Is it possible to bring
something brand-new from essence into form, even
though no one seems to have done it before? What
if my idea-vision-dream is too unique, too out-there?*

Allowing your sacred calling to come into the
bright light of your loving consciousness requires
you to realize that you will be treading the path not
taken. You will be invited into the unknown. But
the reward is an experience of true homecoming,
a fulfillment of the life you were born to live, not a
replica of someone else's.

Following that inner voice inviting you into the
unknown to create a form in the world—a business,
a social initiative, a practice, or an endeavor that
could actually pay the bills while making a major
impact in the lives of others—requires you to source
your ambition and power from what is sacred.

This is what sacred ambition is: birthing your
sacred calling from essence into form from the
blessing or sacredness of you.

The Process

There is no place your sacred calling will not take you. You
will revisit unhealed parts of your past so you can mine the
depths of who you are and claim what you discarded long
ago. You will make friends with aspects of yourself that
you thought were not redeemable and cash in on their fresh
energy. You will learn to be comfortable with the uncomfortable and trust the unknown. And you will redefine and

align power and ambition to what is sacred to you.

Your sacred calling will also use everything that is part of you: all the wins of your life and all the losses. All the hurts from the past—the disappointments, heartaches, and failures—will be transformed by the alchemical process of turning your "lead," through your compassionate loving, into your "gold."

You will go through this process many times, and each time you will know yourself, trust yourself, and fulfill more of who you are. Each rebirth, each spiritual experience that emerges, will find you more complete, more whole, and more *you*.

If you want to hold on to certainty, the known, the status quo, the security of your day-in-and-day-out comfortable, predictable life, you will be challenged. You may have the desire to live your sacred calling, but if the risk of failure—or failure itself—is your personal taboo, that fear will always supply you with convenient excuses to put it off.

You will discover the ways your human nature, your humanity, does not support what it takes for you to follow a sacred calling. But you can learn new reference points for yourself so your human nature can assist, rather than resist, your intention to enter this bigger playing field of self-expansion, personal growth, and soul-revelation.

If you need constant validation or acknowledgment from the world that you are on the right path, you will also be challenged. Knowing who you are at the very depths of your being is one of the first requirements for being able to hear and follow a sacred calling. The outer world is not designed to pat you on the back or fill your cup of approval. Instead, it throws all manner of obstacles and bright, shiny objects in your way to distract you from—or even persuade you to abandon—what is most precious inside. It beckons you to give up this Looney Tunes pie-in-the-sky vision and to join the ordinary masses doing ordinary work in their ordinary lives. But if you learn to listen to your inner guidance and find the outer support necessary, you will resist the world's point of view and learn the systems, strategies, and inner tools that will help you find your way.

You will change how you perceive reality. This process will shake the very foundations of what you believe about yourself, about life, about using power and ambition. Instead of trying to belong and fit in, you will learn to be loyal to your sacred calling—loyal to the True Self of *you*. And this will be your shift in reality: You will see through the eyes of your True Self and observe the world through the lens of compassion, acceptance, loving, and highest good. Your True Self does not deal in competition, striving for success, self-shame and blame, or the old paradigm of being "the king of the mountain."

Is it your time to step out of that comfortable, secure hiding place within and bring your precious blessing forward so all of us can be profoundly touched by the dream in your heart? I say yes!

Throughout this book I sprinkle in stories that give you snapshots of how sacred callings might emerge for you. But this volume is not intended to be a storytelling book. It is written to shine the light brightly on the journey ahead with practical insights, how-tos, and hard-earned wisdom.

My heart's desire is that you find the courage and conviction you need to claim what is most precious within you, declare it—even if it's a whisper—to the part of you that is always listening for you to speak your truth, and take your first seemingly small, yet actually quite big, step.

The world is *ready*.

PART ONE

Sacred Callings

The sacred in you is a blessing—
a blessing to give and a blessing to receive.

CHAPTER One

A Sacred Calling: What Is It?

A SACRED CALLING IS A SUMMONS FROM THE HEART. IT invites you to the truth of who you are and beckons you to express that truth in your life. Sacred callings consist of your True Self, your essence, your very soul. They are revealed to you when you are ready to live your life with more vitality, more commitment, more truth, and more loving.

Callings are sacred because they bring a blessing. You are blessed because you recognize and live your sacred calling, and we are blessed because you shine the light of your calling brightly so that we can see, by your light, more of who we are.

Sacred callings can be ignored, but there is a price to pay. The price is something only you can assess, but part of your life will be unfulfilled if your sacred calling is not acknowledged and claimed.

A sacred calling emerges from deep stirrings of the heart. Sometimes it is a longing that has been whispering for eons, urging you to wake up. Sometimes, like a bolt of lightning, it awakens you in one startling moment of clarity.

Sacred callings can slay your heart, leaving you dazed by the enormity of what you are called into.

Co-creating heaven on earth; ending world hunger; restoring the earth's natural ecosystems; saving the wild places; protecting the children, the animals, the coral reefs—these are not trifling callings that even can be manifested completely in one lifetime. The scale of some callings can be humbling. But the invitation is real. Discovering the part of you that is being asked to show up and contribute is vital.

Sacred callings sometimes emerge from what breaks your heart. Sometimes they bubble up from the depths of your joy. But they always come from inside of you.

How Sacred Callings Show Up: A Defining Moment

Like the flash of a hummingbird's wing that catches your attention for a mere heartbeat or a whiff of a scent on a breeze that momentarily transports you to a different place and time, sacred callings can appear in the oddest moments and in the oddest ways.

You could be twenty-nine years old and in the middle of one of life's many disillusionments—another relationship that didn't work out, a job that didn't come through—and yet beyond all the hurt and disappointment, something else suddenly draws your attention, as if someone whispered, "Look over here." The pain of the hurt wants to distract you from the "something" you just saw that caused your heart to leap in a moment of recognition. But you saw it. And a part of you registered it. In that moment, curiosity was seeded, and from that seed a quest can begin.

You could be forty and facing a divorce or a loss or a shattering of your life as you've known it to be up until that moment, when you cry out, "How did I get here?" And then, quite unexpectedly, you have this awareness: "I feel more real." Something awakens what was asleep, and then a thought follows: "I am going to start over with more of me present." Resiliency is sparked, and from that spark a heart fire begins to ignite.

You could be fifty-five with your last child having packed her bags and left for college or for that backpacking trip in Europe, and you are looking around at emptiness— both outside and inside. The first inklings of the question "What do I do with the rest of my life?" begin to tickle something awake. You could get distracted by filling the emptiness with busyness, but something else is asking you to remember how much you loved, before you had children, to paint or write or play the piano. Suddenly the emptiness transforms into spaciousness, and you expand with it. An excitement bubbles up. And possibilities seem endless.

Or you could be sixty-five and realizing after a successful career that there is more you want to contribute, more you want to express with your life. What legacy will you leave for your children? Your grandchildren? Those you love? What is the inner rave you find yourself voicing inside while showering in the morning, the one that fires every cell alive in your body? What breaks your heart? And what is the unique gift that you can bring to this urgent call?

What all of these defining moments have in common is that the first delicate shoots of a sacred calling appear alongside a life event that could feel like a blow from a two-by-four. In those moments when things are falling apart, what has been hidden in plain sight can finally be revealed and seen. In our regular, controlled, everything-is-flowing-nicely day, we don't sit still long enough to turn inward and observe a fresh idea or feeling. Often we are in too much of a hurry to find something that we hope will entertain us or ease the pain. These distracting activities can drown out a gentle whisper or suppress an inner nudge from beyond the ordinary.

Sacred callings do not attempt to try to get your attention during your hurried, fast-paced life. Why bother? So a metaphorical two-by-four is wielded—out of the blue, or so you believe—to stun you long enough to shift you out of your conditioned routine. But such convergent moments, where the past, present, and future collide, can be painful. Buried unresolved issues, present looming problems, and worries about the future can all hit you at the same time. Your response to this convergence will determine whether you contract and shut down or expand into the opportunity.

+ Will you care enough to finally stop and be present with that pain, numbness, hurt, disappointment, or fear long enough to hear the message your resistance has been masking?

+ Will you take care of yourself in that moment and not dismiss, run from, or negate the true essence and blessing of who you are, which may have been abandoned long ago?

+ And will you finally bring that caring back to where it belongs—to your heart and soul—and be loyal to the divine birthright that is yours if you would only claim it?

Playing Hide and Seek: How Sacred Callings Emerge

When invited to share stories detailing their first awareness of having a calling, people often say, "It's been hiding in plain sight all of my life."

"I always knew I had a powerful connection to the theater."

"I felt for a long time that I had a specific work or mission to take on, although what it was eluded me."

"I was nineteen years old when I heard a voice behind me that said, 'You are going to be a pastor.' It freaked me out, and I said, 'Not me!'"

"I have always known that I had a calling, and I thought that having one was special. What changed was realizing that this is true for everyone."

"I can see now that I was called from the time I became a conscious young adult."

Sometimes they receive a clear inner directive: "You are going to take this light out into the world and help others like yourself."

A calling can also emerge gradually, quietly, and begin to take form later in life, as the pieces of your old existence are rearranged and a new vision appears.

The calling can be tied to a bigger vision of service, either to a cause or to specific group of people in need. Callings use your natural talents and abilities, what you love to do: storytelling, theater, movement, painting, creativity, coaching, teaching, public speaking, inspiring people, creating community, business strategy, marketing. Nothing is wasted and everything is put to use as a calling begins to emerge.

When sacred callings are starting to come forward, like those first green shoots of spring, you'll want to pay attention and move with care so you honor the delicate nature of this time. Patience is required. It is important to ask yourself some bigger questions and answer them honestly:

✦ Does this calling scare me? Or is it challenging me in some way? If so, how?

✦ Am I holding myself back? If yes, why and in what ways?

✦ Am I uncomfortable? If so, with what?

✦ Am I masking fear? If yes, in what ways am I doing it and why?

✦ What do I need to do to continue to allow this calling, which has been singing in my heart for many years, to come forward fully into expression?

✦ What is the blessing for me and for the world?

Take care at this stage to find the inner and outer support you need to feel safe and seen in what may only be a glimpse of your calling. Or if you already have the full picture, the work is more about inner support—learning the tools that will assist you when the inner demons want to squelch that precious vision.

In the emergent stage we often want to move into action too soon. If there is a form of expression as your calling is stirring awake, and you can see it serving the greater good (like a business or social initiative), rushing too soon into creating those business cards or that website can interrupt a deeper incubating process that will make all the difference later. There will be plenty of time for the details.

For now, you must accept that you are in a time of emergence. What does that look like? It could be clearing all the inner baggage around limiting beliefs and fears. It could also include developing a stronger connection to your inner guidance.

All of this will be addressed in a later chapter.

One of the most important choices you make at this time is to find outer support in a group or mentor who knows the territory and can walk with you through this emergent process toward your sacred ambition. Sacred ambitions arising from sacred callings are not birthed in isolation.

Finding your voice and the words to speak and acknowledge your sacred calling—being witnessed and acknowledged, seen and heard—can be the first liberating steps you take.

When Your Sacred Calling Is Not for the World

Here is a good question to ask yourself at this time: *Is my sacred calling for the world?* Not all sacred callings are. Some focus on you—to live your best life through knowing who you are and accepting yourself completely; to be a great friend, mate, or parent; to contribute to your community in a behind-the-scenes way by supporting those who feel called to the front lines. Holding a strong energy of loving, compassion, integrity, honesty, or balance is a wonderful contribution to the greater good and a beautiful sacred calling. Not all of us want to put a stake in the ground for a new paradigm or radical change. Your gifts may be simpler, perhaps, but no less needed. A sacred calling can be to become the best you—to know yourself, to experience more self-loving and self-compassion, and to model that experience for your friends and family.

A great gift you can give to yourself, to your family, and to the world is being an energizing battery of loving, compassion, kindness, and generosity. It is really OK if you prefer not to stand in the spotlight or you don't have the next big idea to change the world. Being you is enough.

When Your Sacred Calling Is for the World

If you have decided that your sacred calling is indeed for the world, listening to your calling and following its guidance is important at this time. The calling will lead you to your next best step. What would support you to create the thriving business, social initiative, or creative project that your heart is calling you to? Or if you already have your business or initiative in place, how could you introduce your sacredness into your livelihood?

If you are just beginning, the most important place to start is establishing a solid foundation within yourself. Otherwise, the world can take you off course easily with its illusions and seductive traps of bright, shiny objects. Sacred callings that evolve into sacred ambition businesses, social initiatives, or creative expressions must be followed from the inside out. And a strong inner container of resilience, courage, self-confidence, self-trust, self-acceptance, and self-compassion is needed to allow them to thrive and flourish in the world.

You must learn to choose the truth of who you are over the stories you keep telling yourself about your flawed life and shortcomings. And you will become intimate and comfortable with uncertainty and the unknown. Otherwise, you will abandon ship even though it's not sinking.

Sacred callings serve the greater good. To live and work in service to the greater good, you will need a solid inner foundation based on a compassionate approach to all the inner challenges that will arise when you step out with your vital work.

You must also have in place the best practices that allow the expression of that sacred calling to flourish, but (and this is important) those practices need to resonate with the inner guidance you are following. When the next "best" way to grow your business or to reach more people is trotted out onto the world stage by a well-known business guru, you will need to use discernment and choose wisely. If you don't, you may become discouraged by what isn't working as you try to follow someone else's model or blueprint. Discouragement can damage your inner container and also send you down a rabbit hole of self-shame and blame.

Then there's the issue of what you truly want. Is it more money? Recognition and fame? Self-fulfillment? Or...? These are all good questions, arising from a place of inner inquiry that is essential to choosing, claiming, and following a sacred calling—and everything that goes with it. To go the distance, you must be aware of your deeper why. In other words, it could be that increasing your yearly gross income is a motivator, but what is your deeper incentive? What experience do you want? More freedom? A greater sense of sovereignty? Space to travel and spend more time with those you love? If your sacred calling presents itself earlier in life, you may decide to put it aside for a while because your plate is too full. But please know that if it doesn't leave you alone, your life will not feel right or on track until you address and make room for what is prodding you for attention.

The important thing here is to recognize that the restlessness in your life—or a recent job loss or your relationship dissolving—may be happening to you because of a long-forgotten vision that won't let you go. Whatever it may be, you have a wonderful opportunity to pause, listen inside, and ask yourself if you are finally going to clear the space to pursue that dream.

So take a moment and declare, based on your best guess, where you are in this emergent stage as you begin to answer and follow your calling—and then be prepared for what may appear. The energy might shift for you suddenly, and you could find yourself not putting off your dream any longer.

CHAPTER TWO

The Wisdom of Folly

IN 2010 I WAS RESTLESS. A PART OF ME WAS FEELING confined, like I had grown out of something and hadn't bought my new size yet.

And I wasn't clear what was going on.

For twenty years I had made steady progress in building a viable spiritually focused counseling practice. I published my first book, *You Can Make It Heaven*, in 2002 and spent two years traveling, giving talks, and leading workshops. In 2005 I began teaching my Heaven on Earth Wisdom School curriculum, which gave me a deep experience of assisting others in opening up to their own divine True Self. And in 2007 I added the Noetic Balancing Practitioner Training, for professionals who wanted to learn how to clear and balance the subtle energy fields.

By 2010 I had a full teaching schedule and private practice working with individuals and couples. So why was I restless?

One day, early in that year, a client brought in a book on crop circles. His fascination with these temporary grain temples caught my attention, and suddenly I heard myself saying out loud: "I want to take a group this summer to England, teach a workshop, and play in the crop circles."

This spontaneous declaration caught me by surprise. And the part of me that was feeling restless sat up straight and said, "Hell, *yeah,* let's do this!" So that summer I found myself boarding a plane to England to lead a workshop, called Co-creating a New Reality, with a small group of enthusiastic participants.

Clearly a new reality was beginning to peek over the horizon at me, and I had a sneaking suspicion that getting out of my cushy comfort zone and walking in these crop formations would finally allow me to shed the old constricting skin so I could breathe freely and deeply.

That this crop circle trip had anything to do with what was next for me in my career did not reveal itself right away. At the time, I was following a heart call. I was full of curiosity and wonder. I wasn't thinking about my counseling practice or whether it needed to change in any way. What was beckoning to me was a new experience of reality and a new perception of what was possible.

This sojourn—into the lush, green, rolling pastures of the Salisbury Plain to hunt for formations created by some inexplicable energy that was mysteriously bending stalks of grain—would change everything.

When I came home from that trip, I was expanded. My vision felt bigger. The confining walls that had limited my inner view of what was possible were gone. I had seen and put my body inside something that my rational mind could not explain. And the effects of this in my consciousness would be revealed more fully a year later, almost to the day.

In the summer of the next year, I took a huge leap and joined a high-powered mastermind group that required plunking down more money than I had ever dreamed was possible. An emerging sacred calling was asking me to take my work to a bigger audience, which meant I myself had to get bigger and come out of hiding. In the months following my crop circle trip, the restless voice inside had become loud and obnoxious. Daily dialogues would go something like this:

Loud obnoxious voice: *It is time.*

Time for what? I'd say in a cheeky way.

Time to break out of this small, comfortable life you have created. Time to take some risks and step out in a bigger way.

So what will happen if I step out and fail? I'd shoot back.

What will happen if you don't? (I told you this voice was obnoxious.)

Well, Rebecca, I'd then ask myself, *what will happen if I don't?*

When I thought about *not* going for whatever this was, a horrifying feeling would immediately come over my body and create a loud "No!" inside. So instead I said, *"Hell, yes!"* even though I didn't know what I was saying yes to.

That is when I knew that the insistent, loud, and (yes) obnoxious voice was not only right, it was the sentinel at the gate patiently beckoning me to stop putting off the life I was born to inhabit.

Folly or Freedom

Stepping into crop circles was stepping into the unknown. So was joining a high-powered mastermind group. I bounced back and forth inside my head, from the thought that these choices of mine were pure folly to the feeling of excitement that I would find a key to a hidden treasure trove of magic and wonder.

Both turned out to be true. Folly is definitely our friend when it allows a sacred calling to send its roots deeper into our consciousness. In fact, at times like these, the rational mind can be a hindrance. When inspiration strikes out of the darkness, it is not a time to be practical. Of course, I had to think about some practical things, but I never questioned the original flash of inspiration.

Folly asks us to suspend our usual day-to-day scheduled life, to walk off the beaten path, to zig and zag more, rather than take the shortest route from A to B. Folly can unfurl a secret sail that catches a wandering breeze and takes us away from our controlled selves toward vistas that light up inner landscapes hidden in a darkness that may be a bit foreboding.

Sure, the traditional opinion of folly is not flattering. It is seen as frivolous, irresponsible, risky, maybe even a bit insane. It can sound fun and exciting but also dangerous.

I was aware of all that when I decided to see if this so-called frivolous trip to England to walk in crop circles would shake up my don't-rock-the-boat life. I also was aware that my mastermind investment was a risk. I had poured my savings (and then some) into an intangible, way-bigger-than-me, overwhelming, unknown calling.

But I was following the voice of my heart, not my rational mind, and the biggest danger I could imagine was that I would not go for it and play it safe instead.

A sacred calling was emerging, and I knew that if I didn't step out of my known life, I would not experience something fresh and maybe even surprising. So for the next eighteen months I followed folly. I made choices that felt risky, unfamiliar, uncomfortable, even bizarre.

And my folly paid off—but not right away.

Dealing with the Inner Critic and Voices of Self-Doubt

There was inner work I had to attend to. The wheels were coming off my life.

As I pursued a new business model, my sense of how I wanted to work with people in the future was also morphing. That meant I no longer saw myself as a traditional counselor. I was faced with the terrifying choice to shut down my traditional one-on-one counseling practice, which paid the bills. My ego-mind wanted desperately for me to abandon this new journey into uncharted waters. It was not happy that I was shifting my business model away from my stable practice, nor did it see how my financial life was going to stay secure while I learned new ways to teach my Wisdom School curriculum online or grow my reach and build a following from scratch outside my small hometown pond.

At one point I flashed on the distinct image that everything I had created and fashioned over the past twenty-one years was in pieces on the floor. They would not fit back together, and I had no clue how to form something new.

The wisdom I was hearing from my well-meaning mastermind gurus was based on their experience of best practices, but each time I tried to follow their advice, something inside did not resonate. And I knew it. Whatever was calling me into a bigger playing field did not fit their model. I was back at square one. And my faith in myself was shaking.

I managed to keep my boat afloat—or at least above water—during a choppy period of sleepless nights peppered with visions of financial ruin. This is when I learned firsthand the importance of not trying to birth a never-been-tried-before sacred ambition business from a new sacred calling without support and inner guidance.

I knew I needed help, but it was imperative that it was the right kind of help. Trying to hide my disaster scenarios behind a strong outer mask of "I've got this" wasn't working. When sacred callings are emerging, we must take care to secure the tried-and-true inner resources that help us navigate those dark moments of self-doubt and visceral fear. I was fortunate to have created a solid foundation: I already knew how to quiet and calm the parts of me that were freaking out and how to clear old limiting beliefs about security and safety. So I began to help myself using the inner tools I had practiced for so many years.

I created a safe inner place of compassion and self-acceptance where I could be with any part of me that was panicking or that felt completely lost and unable to speak. I listened with compassionate ears of acceptance, relaxing into simply being with myself. Vulnerability was my friend. My face relaxed, and so did the tight knot in my stomach.

I surrounded myself with others who were wrestling with their own emerging callings, and together we formed a pact of mutual respect, kindness, and comradery. I was not alone. My shoulders relaxed.

I found a mentor who listened deeply—beyond the siren songs of fast cash, fame, and fortune—to what really needed to be heard. Ever so slowly all those scattered pieces of my career and my gifts and talents began to reform themselves into a new holographic image that my mentor helped me articulate and claim. My anxiety lifted.

And I challenged the part of me that wanted to give myself a back door—a way to quietly and secretly slip away with excuses and rationalizations that maybe this was not the right timing, that maybe all this anxiety and fear was an indication that I was on the wrong track. I quickly discovered that if I allowed myself to entertain this seeming voice of reason and buy its version of my current reality, my inspiration, energy, and focus became muddled.

There were many days when I wanted to quit. Many sleepless nights of "What have I done?!" could not be ignored. But what was bigger than my fear and self-doubt was the sensation of complete devastation in my heart when I considered giving up on what I could not yet name but clearly wanted to be manifested.

So I closed the back door—and bolted it shut. I didn't give myself a way out. I reached out to others. I took a step every day, even if shaky, in the direction of what felt on-point for me. I dug deeper into the inner reserves of self-trust, self-acceptance, and self-compassion. I challenged limiting beliefs and scary fears of what-ifs and held them at bay. I listened more to my inner voice of guidance and truth and followed the guidance that was given. And I let go—of needing to prove myself, of other's opinions, of the world's definition of success, and of business gurus' how-to blueprints that didn't resonate with who I was or who I served.

My story is personal to me, but it contains some common elements that show up over and over for anyone who decides to take their sacred calling seriously.

The Curveballs

Once you make that decision for yourself and pursue what's next—BAM! Here come the curveballs. Here come the voices of self-doubt, distrust, disbelief, and old ingrained messages. *Do I have what it takes? I'm not good enough. Who am I to bring this to the world?*

The anxiety begins to rise.

Sacred callings inevitably take you into the weeds. They set you on a path of a profound inner journey, demanding that you face and feel your deepest fears, step into the unknown, and discover an untapped reservoir of inner trust, inner resiliency, and the deeper blessings of realizing your True Self.

And how will you discover these blessings?
You must do your inner work.

Taking an inner approach to that outer vision you hold is the only way to stay grounded and unshakable when the winds of self-doubt and fear arise. For some, this can be an easy next step. These people are already accustomed to diving into their inner levels and feel comfortable looking under rocks and in dark corners. For others, the inner work is brand-new—uncharted territory, for sure, and maybe a bit intimidating. Perhaps some may have a belief that this aspect of the journey is a waste of valuable time. But please know that if you are not doing your inner work, you are not answering the call, for the sacredness of your True Self—the blessing of who you are—lies within.

The way you deal inside with the challenges that surface
is as important, if not more important, than the
outer steps you take.

Because if you don't deal with these challenges,
you won't take those outer steps.

Sacred callings consistently take you by the hand and direct you back inside. It's the inner work that makes it possible for you to live and express that calling in the world. Callings go silent if we don't create safety within for all voices to be heard, acknowledged, and honored. All those voices—the ones of inspiration and vision and the ones of self-doubt and fear—are part of what is emerging. Each cry for help is asking you to know yourself in a greater way, to know the truth of who you are.

And knowing who you are is a treasured discovery.

The Importance of Finding the Treasure of *You*

The treasure of who you are—your sacredness—does not live in a religious book, although the wisdom found there can inspire you and point to markers along the way. It does not reside in the words of a great spiritual teacher, although teachers can open up levels of your consciousness so you can experience an expanded reality of who you are. It resides in you, as you, being you—all one-hundred percent of you.

No more hiding? No more hiding.

No more pretending? No more pretending.

No more posing? No more posing.

You, as you, being you, one-hundred percent, is a sacred prayer to the divine. You are a living, breathing, laughing, crying, shouting, loving holiness.

"So why don't I know this?" you might ask.

Because you have a lot of clutter in the way. In the crowded closet of your heart, you have stuffed life's hurtful experiences on top of your sacredness. You have vowed, "Never again." You have piled high all the right reasons to use your past loses to obscure and deny who you are. And you have discarded parts of yourself, important parts, and thrown them in the back of the closet, hoping to never see them again.

But have you noticed that cluttered closets are hard to close? Bits and pieces keep falling out, much to your dismay. An invitation from your sacred calling to live full-out, to come out of hiding—that's an invitation to open the closet door wide and begin to clear the clutter.

As sacred callings evolve into sacred ambitions, this is the important work that must be done. Otherwise, you will find yourself abandoning your dream or sabotaging your forward momentum.

This inner work requires you to challenge the limiting beliefs and negative chatter in your head and clear it out. If you don't, you will be defeated before you ever begin.

In chapter nine I go into some detail about my approach to clearing out what will easily sabotage even the greatest of visions and dreams. The approach in this book is just one of many good strategies out there. But please know that ignoring your inner work—even if you have done years of counseling or taken umpteen workshops—can swamp you and put out that heart fire.

Plus, the treasures of your True Self are found in the deeper waters, not strewn across the surface. If you dare to follow your sacred calling and bring that vision into form, you will be challenged and you will be tested.

And one of the biggest tests is being *all-in*.

Chapter Three

The Necessary Hard Lessons
of Being All-in

First, you must respond to the call and accept, rather than resist, that you are being called, that the call is real, and that you will be moving beyond your comfort zone to answer that call. The next step is to commit to it— to be *all-in*.

Commitment. Now there's a word that can elicit all manner of backpedaling. Why is commitment such a scary next step?

Commitment involves dedication, devotion, allegiance, and loyalty. When you are committed to a blazing heart calling, you might wonder, "What is this calling going to ask of me?"

In my forties I wanted to start singing in public again. Growing up I had sung in church choirs, in musicals, and on stage at various events. Singing was a big part of my life that brought me much joy. So I contacted three talented musicians and invited them to an informal jam session. Instantly we all knew we wanted to start a musical group and dedicate it to spreading light and love.

We were all-in. From the first rehearsal we practiced twice a week. We booked engagements in spiritual communities around New Mexico, sang almost every Sunday at a popular spiritual church, gathered the funds to record a cassette tape of our original songs, and wrote music, laughed, practiced, and had fun together—for about eighteen months. And then things began to fall apart.

One of our members began coming late to rehearsals or missing them altogether. Excuses were made about why this particular song wasn't going well. Performances got a bit sloppy. Egos began to speak up about the order of songs in our concerts and who sang which song. Feelings were hurt. Our hundred-percent commitment began to fray.

By the time we sat down to talk about what was going on, one of our members had one foot out the door. What was hard for me was that I still wanted to hold things together. I tried to convince the members that this was just a phase and that we could rekindle our initial spark.

But I could feel the energy leaving the group.

So we gave our farewell concert and went our separate ways.

The breakup was painful for me. I was still attached and not wanting to let go. Why wasn't my commitment enough?

But it was through that experience that I learned a valuable lesson about commitments. While I could still be highly invested, I also needed to be unattached to the outcome.

Commitment to following a sacred calling wherever it may lead requires you to be all-in but unattached.

Holding both of those approaches when you are a hundred percent committed is a dance of giving it everything and at the same time letting go. It forces you to remember that sacred callings serve the highest good, not our individual, ego-personality, the-way-I-want-it good.

Sacred callings cannot be fooled. If you secretly give yourself a way out from the get-go, if you say you are devoted and dedicated to your sacred calling with your fingers crossed behind your back, the part of you that knows your truth will not be fooled. And, consequently, that one percent you are holding back could prevent you from discovering hidden treasures of who you are and possibly a major life fulfillment.

Mary's Story

Mary felt lost. But who wouldn't be reeling after two cancer diagnoses and the realization that her thirty-four-year career as a travel agent and international tour guide was coming to an end.

It was Mary's choice. She knew that the travel, the workload, and the business didn't serve her any longer. She was grateful for all the wonderful people she had met and the exciting places she had visited around the world. "I have literally been around the world so many times in thirty-four years," said Mary. "What a blessing."

But when she mentioned to a friend that she felt spiritually lost thinking about completing this part of her life and uncertain about her future, the friend suggested she might find a new direction by attending an event I was hosting, called Your Sacred Ambition.

"My experience attending the event was eye-opening," Mary recalled. "Instead of the fear and heaviness that I had been experiencing, I started to see new possibilities, and new energy of excitement came rushing in. And I allowed myself to articulate a dream that I had been holding for some time at the event. WOW! What a rush of energy that was. I knew in that moment that my dream was a sacred calling. I got this by realizing that the idea was given to me as a spiritual message."

Mary's spiritual message was to start a new business organizing LGBT weddings in New Mexico. "I was clear about my new business but had never considered it a sacred ambition. I discovered during the Sacred Ambition event that this new business was indeed a calling much deeper than I had imagined."

So Mary acknowledged her calling. But did she accept it fully and commit to being all-in?

Mary had questions and a lot of fear. "I have put aside some money to last me till next fall," she remembered telling herself, "but if I quit the travel business and next fall gets here but I haven't made any money, then what?"

She kept getting pulled into F.E.A.R.—Future Expectations Appearing Real. She was going for her dream business ninety-nine percent rather than a hundred percent—and that was a bitch.

Mary had one foot on the accelerator and one foot on the brake. When she was home in between her trips, she dove headlong into her new sacred ambition business—building her new website, making contacts, reaching out to potential clients—but her back door was wide open. When the call came to take just one more travel job, her fear had her saying yes—not a *"Hell, yes!"* but an *"I-don't-want-to-do-this-anymore-but-I'm-afraid yes."* And this yo-yoing was costing her, big time.

When she was away traveling, she completely lost her hold on the energy of her calling, so the process of coming home was bumpy. She had to fight her way back to a place of inner calm and trust. When she and I finally had a chance to address this situation, Mary felt like she was losing the battle.

"What is it going to take," I asked her, "to close the back door and begin trusting your inner guidance? If one-hundred percent commitment is a *"Hell, yes!"*—and much easier than being at ninety-nine percent, almost all-in—what is your *"Hell, yes!"*?

For Mary it was getting in touch with what she truly wanted—her big *why*—what she knew in her soul was missing from her life and would make all the difference. Mary wanted to experience more joy, and when she realized that creating her sacred ambition business was all about joy—well, ta-da!—she got to her *"Hell, yes!"*

One year later...

After giving her new business her attention off and on for about twelve months, Mary realized that along with joy she also had to have security. Staying with a new business that might not pay the bills was too uncertain.

So she ended her commitment to her new business venture and signed back on as a full-time travel concierge.

Not the ending to this story that you expected?

When Mary finally got to her *"Hell, yes!"* she began to hear from parts of herself that she didn't want to admit were there. She allowed her deeper fear to have a voice. Yes, she wanted more joy in her life, but her joy was not tied to what she was doing so much as to how she took care of what was even more important to her—her inner sense of security. When that was in place, so was her joy.

We all have different levels of ability to deal with uncertainty, and for Mary that tolerance had been reached. She needed to get back on solid ground, and the known world of the travel business was where she could feel the ground underneath her again.

But the key learning that surfaced—the unexpected blessing of her sacred calling—was *how* she went back to the travel business.

"I did not shame myself for my fear," she said. "This was huge! I did not blame myself for not sticking with my new vision longer. I was very compassionate with those parts of me that were saying loudly, 'This is too scary for us. We need the security of a consistent pay check.'" During the year that Mary had dedicated to her new business venture, she had been doing her inner work—creating a new foundation based in self-loving and self-compassion. And this, she discovered, allowed her to listen to the voices of fear without making herself wrong or feeling like a failure.

Mary renewed her relationship with her inner guidance. "I make time every day to tune in and listen inside. And I see my role now traveling all around the world as an ambassador of peace and goodwill, and that makes me very happy."

Aha! So her sacred calling brought her a surprising opportunity to bring forward her heart and service anyway. And her ability to access greater security expanded. She now had the inner security of knowing she could love herself no matter what. Her sacred calling turned out to be more about her inner development than about creating a new sacred ambition business.

Did Mary have any regrets? "I know I didn't give my new business everything. But I also know that if I didn't have money in the bank, I could not feel my joy."

Did she learn anything else? "Absolutely. I know myself so differently now. I know what really makes me happy, and I also am so in touch with my inner guidance. Yes, I am working in the travel industry again, but I am doing it differently, with joy. And it is making all the difference."

The results of being all-in while following a sacred calling can be surprising. It doesn't necessarily guarantee that the original vision of a new business venture or career path will come to fruition. Who knew that Mary would discover a surprising way to share her blessing? She now has a renewed enthusiasm and gratitude for all the amazing adventures she continues to experience while traveling around the world.

What a great sacred calling!

Chapter Four

Avoiding Traps and Detours

I HAVE TALKED ABOUT THE IMPORTANCE OF BEING ALL-IN, because even when we declare we have both feet on the path, that is no guarantee our initial vision will manifest.

Patience with how our sacred calling wants to emerge is another challenge we might encounter when we are deep in the inner excavation phase, wondering if all the time spent is really worth it.

But there are other traps and detours. I know. I have experienced them all. As sacred callings turn into sacred ambitions, there are three common traps to anticipate. If ignored or dismissed, they can rob you of your passion, your energy, and your resolve.

TRAP #1: Playing Small to Be Accepted and Fit In

This trap shows up when you are in the delicate stage of taking those first wobbly steps out into the world with your great work. Or you have decided to go full steam ahead and create that website, design those business cards, rent that storefront, write that blog, invite your first clients ...

and then you stop in your tracks. What happened to your inspired momentum?

Suddenly you have lost the heart of what you were doing, and you begin to question yourself. *What will people think about this new direction in my life? Will they laugh at me? What if I don't fit in anymore?*

This trap can feel like a war within yourself. You may feel a conflict between the desire to put yourself out there and the pull of that insidious inner critic that keeps saying, "You're just not good enough." Perhaps you are torn between the needs of your family and the work of your sacred ambition. Maybe you want to be a powerful business leader but are afraid you won't be accepted.

Sadly, you have few (if any) role models who can show you how to be ambitious and powerful in a way that is attractive and aligned with the integrity of your True Self. As a bright, intelligent man or woman who is on a bigger mission, you might feel villainized for trying to stand in your power. And what about the guilt you secretly feel if you don't go for your dreams?

Other subtle ways you could be playing small:

+ Denying and minimizing the importance of what you do

+ Experiencing apathy or ambivalence about wanting to be successful

+ Making excuses about not having enough time, energy, resources, or strategies

+ Harboring limiting beliefs and a fear that you don't have what it takes

TRAP #2: The Bright, Shiny Objects Syndrome

Often you can get caught up in winning or reaching for that elusive standard of achievement, only to find that the cost is way too high. You can spend all your energy making sure everyone else is taken care of except you. You can push yourself out the door in the morning with a long list of to-dos only to find at the end of the week there is still more to accomplish: strategizing for that next income goal, filling that new tele-seminar, finding that next client, trying to figure out how to win and have it all in the right way. Yes, these bright, shiny objects of success—of bigger, more, better, of accomplishment—can lead you on an exhausting chase. It can also feel overwhelming.

And what about those you love? Are you worried they are getting ignored in your push to achieve professionally? Children grow up quickly. Your most precious intimate relationships—with spouses, partners, and other significant people—require attention. And the single most important relationship in your life, your relationship with you, needs time as well. When did you last take real quality time for yourself—to rest, renew, and refresh your body, mind, and soul?

TRAP #3: Ambivalence About Ambition and Power

Perhaps you have dealt with the inner voice of self-sabotage and now feel more confident in stepping out. You know your sacred calling is urging you forward in a big way. You know your ambition and your vision is in service to your calling and the greater good. But you doubt yourself. How do you align your ambition to what is most sacred to you? Do you question whether you have the resources and energy to stay the course? Persistence and continual inspired action are the keys to doing your work with sacred ambition. If you shrink from your True Self, the power of who you are, you set up a repeating loop inside your head that says you are not enough—or, conversely, that you are too much—and you stay small.

Do you wonder if it's OK to have a spiritually focused business, to be a powerful force for change *and* have ambition? Often people are haunted by a time in the past when sharing their heart and soul through their gifts and talents was not safe. You may question whether being a powerful and ambitious man or woman can actually serve the greater good—or what that even means.

In addition to these traps, there are several other ways you can distract yourself and take a detour that could convince you to abandon your big dream too soon.

DETOUR #1: Fear of Taking Risks

Our basic human nature does not like risk. We like comfort. We like what is known and predictable. However, when you want to manifest a sacred calling into a sacred ambition business or social initiative or creative project, the status quo is not going to support you. Realizing this early in your process can bring up fears of taking risks such as speaking out, showing up, and declaring your dream. If you have an aversion to risk, you may end up taking a detour by keeping busy with other seemingly important actions that conveniently cause you to avoid taking the necessary—and sometimes scary—steps to promote your sacred ambition.

DETOUR #2: Your Big Why Isn't Clear or It Fades Away

Wanting to make a difference and leave a legacy is all well and good, but it takes a lot of work and energy. Things can go wrong—and probably will. Finding the time and money to make it work isn't all glitter and rainbows. And all the activity needed to make it work can cause your why to fade into the background, making you more apt to lose your enthusiasm and the energy required to keep persisting.

The actions you take to set up your sacred ambition can also be a detour if you're not guided by your why. So it is imperative to stay in touch with your heart's deepest why, the real reason you're going after that big vision.

DETOUR #3: Insufficient Commitment

Committing to your sacred calling repeatedly is necessary for staying on the road to your sacred ambition. What is your relationship to your sacred calling? Do you hope that simply identifying it will automatically cause your sacred ambition to manifest? Do you merely wish that you might be able to fulfill this calling ... somehow, someday? Or are you truly committed?

There's a subtle but powerful shift that occurs once you are truly committed to your dream. Something galvanizes your energy and your very being. You have shut the back door and announced to the world, "I am going to do this." Until you make that declaration, you don't have a sacred calling that has a prayer of becoming a sacred ambition. You have a pipe dream.

DETOUR #4: Lack of Self-Trust

This is the one thing I hear most often from those just start-ing to bring their sacred calling forward: Can I trust this? Can I trust myself? Keeping your agreements with yourself, saying you are going to take a step and actually taking that step, establishes self-trust. Not following through breaks self-trust and puts you on a major detour—possibly leading to a dead end. It sounds simple, and it is simple. Believing in yourself is crucial on those days when you are the only one carrying the flame. Lack of self-trust destroys so many good ideas and big dreams. And we all lose.

DETOUR #5: Stopping When Things Go Wrong

And they will. The unexpected will arise to take you off course. After all, you are being required to do things you've never done before. Precisely because you don't have evi-dence from the past that you can do this, the inevitable breakdowns and setbacks that arise can seem like proof that you can't do it. It might feel hopeless, and quitting could feel like a viable option. But keep persevering. Stop-ping when things go wrong is not only admitting defeat, but your sacred ambition will never materialize. As you learn from your mistakes, you will discover ways to suc-ceed in performing the necessary tasks—or finding other people who can help you.

DETOUR #6: Trying to Do It by Yourself

You alone can do it, but you can't do it alone. Your sacred calling is unique, but trying to do it all by yourself will lead you on a detour to burnout and leave you precariously vulnerable to giving up. Your first job as the leader of your sacred ambition vision is to find those who resonate with your dream. You may join them or they may join you, but for any initiative to take root in reality requires that you not be the only one sharing that purposeful intent.

DETOUR #7: Not Asking for What You Need

You might hesitate to ask for what you need because you're afraid of sounding pushy or bothering someone. So instead you wish for what you need and end up feeling frustrated and maybe even resentful. Over time this can spell disaster for a sacred calling trying to manifest itself into form. You may find yourself compromising your time, your energy, and your big ideas. This can cause your dreams to come to a slow grinding halt.

DETOUR #8: Lack of Focus and Structure That Creates a Loss of Momentum

Does this sound like you sometimes? You click on Facebook just to see who has posted and then realize an hour has gone by and you've gotten nothing accomplished. Or you are searching for something on the internet and keep getting distracted by first this link and then another. And then you tell yourself you don't have time to allow your sacred calling to emerge.

Following the breadcrumb prompts that beckon you toward inspired action requires focus. Lack of structure and attention to the things that really matter have cost people a loss of momentum, a loss of self-esteem, sometimes years of lost time, and a giving up of their dreams. These common traps and diversions are just a handful of ways you can become driven by your own shortcomings and unhelpful attitudes and lose your way—or worse, give up. They can show up at any stage in the process of bringing your sacred calling forward. However, if you take care to pay attention and be conscious of these traps and challenges, allowing the path of fulfillment to lead you in a manner that honors every part of you, then the greater wisdom of how to proceed will be revealed in ways that may astonish you.

Ultimately, you want to know that your powerful message and ambition can align with what is most sacred within you.

Chapter Five

The Deeper Waters of Your Sacred Calling

THE DEEPER WATERS OF YOUR CALLING DELIVER THE surprise booty that your soul has been safeguarding all of your lifetimes. Have you ever considered that the time vault of your soul's journey harbors secret knowledge, flashes of brilliance, and nuggets of delight? Sacred callings often come with the promise of surprise. Who are you really, as your True Self? And what would your life be like if you sourced that wellspring of treasures?

Bobbye's Story: Building Communion Within

Bobbye had a compelling drive to assist people in bringing their inner life out into the world. "I grappled with how to express this in so many ways over the years," she said. "My sacred calling was all about the inner—waking people up, increasing the level of consciousness in the world and in people, and inviting them to know themselves as a soul and a divine radiant being." But she couldn't figure out whether this calling was a business or a mission or just a conversation over tea.

For a long time Bobbye held on to a belief that the outer world was not ready for what she longed to offer. The groups of people she was a part of— her coworkers at her job, for example—didn't seem interested in waking up consciously or knowing themselves as soul. When she shared her perspective with friends, she got only blank stares in response. Clearly there was a disconnect between what Bobbye was communicating and what people were willing or ready to experience. But gradually she found circles of people who were curious and even wanting what she had to offer. They seemed more open, more willing to explore beyond the safety and comfort of the known.

But she still had not found her tribe.

"One of the most significant dramatic upgrades for me in following my calling was connecting into the sacred ambition tribe," she said. What transpired for Bobbye when she attended her first Sacred Ambition workshop was truly unexpected. "The Sacred Ambition event literally galvanized a life-changing, tectonic shift from Chicago to New Mexico … and it was that community and your teachings—honoring, recognizing, and appreciating the inner part of the journey—that were so incredibly refreshing and resonant for me." She had found a new tribe of support. She had a way to talk about her work that felt resonant and compelling. And she had found a mentor who knew the territory.

Her calling began to form itself around her ambition. With this newfound support, Bobbye could embrace her life's work and invite people to take a stand "for the life-force energies, or chi, of radiant wholeness." Bobbye invited others to play in and "surf the mystery," as she likes to say, so a new story for our time could emerge.

As Bobbye continued to allow the deeper waters of her calling to speak to her, she described her experience as "dancing across the void without a net." And this process was completely OK with her.

Part of bringing sacred callings forward into form is navigating the unknown and the yet-to-be-spoken language that articulates that calling, so others can understand and receive the message. It is a mystery and must be approached with great care. Otherwise, the words fall flat and the magic of resonance and communion does not take place.

This communion requires full embodiment of your sacred calling. It must sing inside of you as you. And you must know how to play the music for those ears that are ready to listen, hear, and respond.

Bobbye's sacred calling of championing the inner way now has a place—as well as a voice, inner and outer support, and a community ready to receive what she wants to give.

Isabel's Surprise Invitation for More Self-Loving

"It was the weirdest thing. I was all geared up to take my business to the next level—and wham! During one of my writing times, up came this memory from the past of one of my deepest, darkest heartbreaks," Isabel said. "Here I was, turning fifty years old, and I couldn't stop thinking about what had happened when I was in my mid-twenties."

Not only did Isabel's memories come flooding back for her, but so did all the shame and grief. They halted any forward movement that she had planned and would not budge until she addressed what she had conveniently locked away so many years ago.

"Now, after months of writing and using tools that I learned to help clear all the self-blame and shame I felt, I can finally get my head above all the deep emotions and see what was really going on here."

Isabel continued: "To move out into the world with more heart passion about my blessing and my sacred calling, I had to have that part of my heart back. To be able to serve my clients from a deeper place, I had to stand against the raging storm of emotions inside me and deal with them."

So she did just that—despite questioning from time to time why, exactly, this memory was surfacing now. In the end, she got it. It was all about a deeper experience of self-loving. Self-loving is so needed when we are living our sacred ambition in the world. Isabel's self-loving gave her the inner strength she needed to expand her sacred ambition business.

Recognize when a sacred calling is knocking on your heart's door, and let it enter. Then honor it gently and hold it lovingly in your heart so it can fully emerge. While you assess what you want to do with all this blazing light, you also need to have the courage to confront and clear the baggage from the past. Clearing this baggage reveals the hidden treasure of the soul's resilience. We discover, that despite the hard knocks and painful heartbreaks, we are whole in our nature as a soul.

Diving deep into the waters of our sacredness and clearing away the dross opens us up to energies and channels that are connected to unlimited possibilities, greater depths of inspiration and creativity, and expansive access to the holiness of the True Self.

We can't force sacred callings to happen. But when we become clear channels of receptivity, they can't help but flow through us and out into the world.

And when that takes place, we can't not do what we are called to.

PART TWO

Sacred Ambition

Success is outer. Fulfillment is inner. You can be successful and not fulfilled. But if you are fulfilled, you will be successful.

CHAPTER SIX

When Sacred Callings
Become Sacred Ambitions

WHEN A SACRED CALLING BECOMES A FORM OR EXPRES-
sion in the world, the inner source that fuels the project,
cause, business, or social initiative is forged in the fire of
your heart's blazing passion. Bringing the sacred calling
to fruition requires you to claim your personal power and
ambition. This process is sacred, for it is imbued with the
blessing of who you are. Each person's process of manifesting their sacred ambition is unique. But the beginning always
requires an inside-out approach.

Realizing You Are Ready

I have to say that when I decided to say *"Hell, yes!"* to that
ambitious inner prompting to bring my sacred calling to a
bigger audience—to change more lives, to alleviate more
unnecessary suffering, and to awaken the inner heaven one
person at a time—I had no idea what it would take or how
it would look.

At first I thought it was just a matter of learning some new online marketing skills: how to write a blog, create a better website, launch a successful webinar series, practice a signature talk, get more likes on my Facebook page, grow my email list, and attract more people to sign up for what I was offering.

At the time of my sacred calling, I had already done years of inner work, published a book, taught my Wisdom School, and had many experiences delivering content and working with individuals and groups. I thought the leap would be small and doable, but the first time I honestly looked at what I was really saying yes to, I did not expect my reaction. I was terrified.

My well-practiced words about who I was and what I did while working with others just fell flat inside. And the online market was getting crowded. How was my voice going to stand out? Reach those I was meant to teach and mentor? The task seemed overwhelming, and my big-fish-in-a-small-pond experience vanished. I was now a small fish in a *huge* ocean—and all the familiar landmarks disappeared.

Piled on top of that, I was about to come out of hiding *big time!* Sacred callings are like that. They shine the light brightly on what is most precious and vulnerable. This felt hazardous. Would I be judged? Ridiculed? Become a target?

Little is written or spoken about the hidden fears and feelings of unsafety that come with being seen and heard when you step out in the full power of who you are. I quickly surmised that all my newfangled bells and whistles of internet marketing and promotion were not going to create the solid place of self-assurance and self-fulfillment that I realized were the hidden gifts of choosing to create a new business from my sacred ambition.

I was going to know myself at a deeper and more authentic level. I was going to face fears that had lain dormant for years—and lifetimes.

My new sacred ambition business was to mentor and teach those who had a sacred calling, to help them know the blessing of who they are by clearing away the clutter of who they are not, and to assist them in claiming their inner personal power and ambition so they could manifest their sacred calling. *And* I wanted to do this on a world stage and increase my income substantially.

The online gurus of the day offered their magic formulas for success and one-size-fits-all courses on how to get more clients and increase revenue streams. But their flashy plans didn't appeal to me, nor would they appeal to those who would be attracted to my approach. After attending their courses for about two years, I realized I was going to have to find my own way on the sometimes dark and barely discernible path to deliver to the world this new sacred ambition business born from the inner calling of my heart.

I had chosen this lifetime to follow a divine blueprint. I also realized that since I could no longer ignore the insistent calling of my heart, I must be ready. Knowing you are ready is an important realization to absorb. If you are being called, you will be supported. If you know this is your time, all manner of unseen forces will move into alignment to illuminate your path. And you will learn—through trial and error—what it is you are really here to fulfill.

Vincent's Story: Taking Himself Seriously

Vincent attended the Sacred Ambition live event in 2016. He allowed himself to listen deeply within. He had given himself the time and space not to run from what was calling him. And for the first time, he took his calling seriously.

This changed everything for Vincent. He said, "I feel like my sacred calling is about being true to myself. By expressing myself, I can heal myself and I can heal others. My experience in the Sacred Ambition event was the first time I allowed myself to take myself seriously and to start manifesting my calling through expressing myself freely."

Vincent developed a sacred calling statement: "To listen to my heart, quiet my mind, love my body, free my spirit, show forgiveness, seek divine guidance, and live out my dreams."

He continued: "I discovered that for a long time there were certain things I wanted to channel and bring into the world, but I didn't believe I deserved to be compensated for that." Vincent had bought into the myth that first you make money, so that when you retire you can finally do what really matters.

"What got connected for me on the third day of the event was that it was absolutely and positively OK for me to bring my gifts to the world and be compensated," he said. "I had to take my calling seriously before anyone else would."

For Vincent this was a huge breakthrough. He had experienced many years of struggle and conflict about money and what he could charge his clients as an entrepreneur. He got to the point where he didn't even want to think, see, or know anything about money in any way—and, of course, that approach didn't work well. He also had a fear that if he had abundance, he would be stupid with his money and waste it rather than be a good steward. This conundrum kept Vincent stuck in a self-defeating loop, one that imprisoned his heart's longing and his creative expression.

But it wasn't making a large amount of money that set him free. It was getting—really getting—that who he was and what he had to offer had great value.

As Vincent put it, "I see now that I have things to offer the world, to improve people's lives: relationships, their mental and emotional states, families, parent-child relationships, and people who are dealing with addictions. And those offerings are worthy of compensation. "He is also learning about being in the present, rather than having his past pull or push his focus away from the moment. He is releasing his money issues and creating a fresh, new relationship with his calling and its ability to generate income.

By clearing past issues that can derail us—like financial fears or lack of trust or not taking ourselves seriously—we can create a present that is rich, exciting, and fulfilling. Then, in turn, we are opened up to a future that's brightly lit by the promise and goodness of who we are.

Vincent's final thoughts: "Now I have the sensation of being pulled forward by the future. On some levels it feels like I am already there—in this future that is full of possibilities. I am gathering together all the different parts of me to claim what is already present."

Staying the Course: Five Key Elements

As your sacred calling matures and you know that soon the birth of an expression of your sacred ambition is inevitable, you must address and actualize five areas to complete the passage from the emergent stage to a smooth process of manifestation.

In order to follow your sacred calling and live it as your sacred ambition business, cause, social initiative, or creative project, you will need these five key elements that enable you to stay the course:

1. Know Who You Are

If you think you know who you are, go deeper. This first element is the keystone that holds all the other elements together. If you skip your inner work and declare that you are done with knowing who you are, you will be undone by what your sacred calling and sacred ambition will ask of you. Even if you have had years of self-examination and lots of inner work, please understand that this inner work is different.

You are a multidimensional being and have layers and levels of clutter that need to surface. In fact, by doing the necessary work of clearing the inner clutter, you earn the right to go to a new level of awakening. It's actually a huge blessing that stuff surfaces as your sacred calling unfolds and your sacred ambition artfully shapes your offering to the world. Here are more opportunities to get free and to expand in your True Self, the loving nature of who you are.

Along with old issues and hurts about ambition and power, other gnarly experiences like disappointment, rejection, abandonment, guilt, and self-doubt can appear seemingly out of nowhere. You may ask yourself, "Why am I dealing with this now? What does this old hurt have to do with my sacred ambition?"

Bringing forward your sacred calling—what is most precious in your heart and soul—requires you to know all of who you are and be able to work with yourself in a loving, compassionate way. Often when you raise the bar and go for what you truly want, some disowned part of you jumps out of the proverbial closet and says, "Hello, you haven't seen me in a while." And your reaction to that can stop you in your tracks.

Here's a short personal account that illustrates how parts of us can show up and surprise us, demanding to be addressed.

Rikki's Story: First Things First

Rikki's life journey had been rich. She had lived in many different parts of the world, held several advanced degrees, and felt accomplished in multiple areas. When Rikki enrolled in my Sacred Ambition Mentorship program, she was unclear about her sacred calling. Rikki remarked: "I know there is something I want to express, but I can't find the words."

As she explored her heart and essence more deeply, what emerged was a knowing that she had kept hidden from herself all her life. The knowing was that she was a divine child of God. Her calling was to own and live that calling.

But what happened next was a surprise to Rikki.

Immediately after claiming her sacred calling, Rikki was confronted inside with an unresolved aspect of her past: her mother leaving her when she was a small child. Why? Because Rikki had to bring home all the abandoned, repressed, frozen, and discarded pieces of herself she had left behind as a result of that experience. If Rikki were to own and live her birthright as a divine child of God, she had to reclaim all those painful but important parts. All of her was divine, not just the aspects she approved or accepted.

It's important to remind yourself on occasion that your inner work is the foundation on which you will build your sacred ambition expression. Ignore the inner work, and the foundation will not hold.

Rikki was courageous. She realized she had made up a story that she was unlovable. She cleared what no longer served her, healed, and brought herself home to herself. Today she has liberated her energy, loving, and focus to express her calling through creative projects and the way she lives her life.

It is folly to say you have already completed all the work you need to do. Instead, be wise and stay present with yourself. In chapter nine I include some inner tools proven to help you shift and clear what no longer serves you.

As you set yourself free, you are a blessing to the world around you. Celebrate!

2. Embrace Uncertainty and the Unknown

The stories I have gathered from sacred ambition leaders, visionaries, and those who spiritually serve others are very similar. From these accounts I have discovered that sacred callings oftentimes showed up initially as vague, unclear, formless messages that they couldn't grasp or put into words—sometimes for years. On top of all this vagueness, sacred callings come packaged with a ticket to the realms of uncertainty and the unknown.

Great. Now what?

Here are a few examples of how that uncertainty can show up:

"I committed myself to the spiritual path but was still 'wandering in the wilderness' for decades ... trying to find the right form of expression."

"My sacred calling awareness fluctuated over the years ... like an antenna that captures radio waves. The reception would shift in and out, so that at times the signal was loud and clear and at other times choppy."

"Sometimes the longing fuels the ambition to create, and at other times I feel like I turn away from it ... and I experience anxiety and frustration and not knowing exactly what shape or form this sacred calling is going to take."

It is unusual for sacred callings to present themselves early in life in full form and expression. But it does happen. Most people, however, experience false starts and stops, alternating between being on the path and off the path, in an impassable thicket. This is why so many abandon the search for clarity. It takes a willingness to sit with a partially-formed sacred calling, embrace it, and wait for the time when it feels defined enough to move out of the shadows and into the light.

Your sacred calling is unique to you. It then follows that you, all of you, must manifest it. If you already knew how to do this, you would have already done it. The path has been created for you to follow, but it goes toward a destination that most of the time is beyond the borders of your comfort zone.

So the key is to learn how to establish new reference points for yourself that bring order in the midst of what might feel like chaos, and a surefootedness when the road gets narrow and rough.

Your human nature will always call you back into what is comfortable and known and puts you in control. Your divine nature, which is the source of all sacred callings, will beckon you to the land of growth, expansion, and self-revelation. To live your sacred calling while you are taking the steps to manifest your sacred ambition expression will require you to grow in your ability to work with yourself in a compassionate way, expand into the greater power of who you are, and allow your sacred calling to reveal to you what it is you truly want.

3. Give Yourself Permission To Do, Be, and Have What You Truly Want

What do you want? I mean really want? At the first transformational workshop I attended, this was the question on day five: "What do you want?"

At that time it seemed like a simple enough question. Isn't it easy to know what I want?

But my experience of that process was much different than I expected.

My vivid memory of that process of asking, "What do I want?" is an image of myself, standing on a chair, shouting as loud as I could with tears streaming down my face, "I want to love!" In fact, I shouted it over and over again—along with a room full of about two-hundred other participants who were also shouting their wants—so much that I lost my voice.

Now, what was that energy that got unleashed during that process so many years ago? What did it break open inside of me? And what happened as a result of that process?

Well, I did discover how to love—not only how to love for the first time but to find out what loving was all about. That experience of love that erupted from the depths of my heart is still at the core of everything I do today. That is the power that comes from giving yourself permission to be, do, and have more of what you truly want.

What you truly want reflects who you are and what you came here to learn, to share, and to bless others with. What you truly want resonates so fully that your entire body vibrates with its energy.

What you truly want you often hide from or deny. Why? Because you ask yourself, "What if I risk everything and go for it, but I don't get it?"

Or, "What if I don't survive the disappointment and despair from not getting what I want?"

So many years are spent going after substitutes, trying to stuff material things into the hole that resulted when you didn't allow yourself to know what you truly wanted. We needlessly waste energy second-guessing and sidestepping ourselves and our desires because of some limiting belief that having what we want is "selfish" or "not spiritual."

When you give yourself permission to be, do, and have what you truly want, the divine power of who you are can flow through you, unencumbered by conditions, limitations, fears, self-consciousness, and self-doubt. This is what we are here to do—find out exactly what it is we truly want and express it, freely, openly, and with as much ambition and power as possible.

So please stop pretending that knowing what you want is not important. Be courageous. Reveal it to yourself. A sacred ambition cannot be served if you don't claim what you want.

4. Cultivate a Thriving Inner Dialogue with Your Divine Guidance

Your relationship with the divine cannot be a casual "I'll call you later" kind of partnership. Divine guidance must be experienced and embodied frequently, so you can recognize it when it shows up, learn how to tune into its energy or frequency, and feel confident weighing the integrity of the intuitive flashes and insights it delivers. Discernment is a tool you must use often when manifesting sacred ambitions, because the world has lots of ways to lure you into squandering your precious resources. It's not necessary to be fearful of the world; it is there to teach you your lessons. But divine guidance is also there to caution you and allow you to learn how to create responsibly.

Prayer, meditation, contemplation, inner listening, inner dialogue, and dreams are excellent ways to explore the channels that your guidance uses to connect with you. Don't limit yourself just to what you are used to. Allow yourself to be attentive and receptive to other avenues of connection and conversation with the divine. You could be walking the dog and an intuitive flash of an image appears that gives you an insight into how to handle a situation. Or as you contemplate your day in the morning shower, you might hear an inner voice that tells you to call someone who can assist you in your sacred ambition. Divine guidance will not intrude, so make it a practice in your day—every day—to invite its blessings.

And then follow through.

It is important to understand that if you continue to receive guidance but don't act on it, you may find your inner companion gradually becoming more and more silent. Inspiration must be followed by inspired action.

Doing does it.

5. Find the Support and Manifestation Strategy that is Right for You

It takes a village of supporters, mentors, coaches, and partners, as well as best practices, to bring your sacred calling forward to serve the greater good. Don't even think you can do this by yourself—you can't. And, even more important, you are not supposed to.

Sacred ambitions are to be shared and expressed as invitations for others to join. This is the time for us to reach out and support the multiple causes promoted by others following their own sacred callings and manifesting their sacred ambitions in the world. If you know of someone besides yourself who has a sacred vision, let them know you see them and champion them to keep taking their steps.

Sacred ambitions must be grounded in good business practices so you can do well—financially, emotionally, spiritually, and health-wise. The better you do, the greater good you can contribute. If making money with your sacred ambition business is essential, apply best practices by learning from those who have led the way. Find the systems and strategies that work for you—and there are many—and keep going.

Good energy begets good energy. And when your energy is generated by the divine loving coming from who you are, that energy is unlimited.

Here are a few examples of the services performed by sacred ambition businesses and social or creative initiatives founded by people I have mentored:

+ Working with highly sensitive women entrepreneurs to grow thriving businesses

+ Helping women in the second half of life to connect to their sacred work, to foster transformation through storytelling

+ Forming circles of women entrepreneurs to help bring more feminine healing energy to the planet

+ Being a poet of divine presence

+ Being a voice and taking a stand for the forgotten women and children of the world

+ Shifting the current business paradigm so that it serves all instead of a few

Sacred ambitions must be thriving, sustainable, and viable businesses or initiatives that support you and the great work you have come to do.

It is time to lift these heart-based initiatives away from the outskirts and plunk them right next to the banks, mortgage companies, real estate offices, grocery stores, and CPA firms on Main Street. The world is hungry for what you have to offer. Your heart and soul focused business can contribute to the common good and provide a model demonstrating that all of who we are as spiritual human beings can be validated and valued.

Stop apologizing for who you are and for that dream in your heart! Build your sacred ambition business or initiative or creative project in a form that works for you, and they will come.

Chapter Seven

Redefining Power

You are a powerful creator, and if you want to manifest your sacred ambition expression, you must claim that power. There's no way around it.

But most of us, when invited to step into our personal power, back away exclaiming, "Oh no, I'm not powerful. People wouldn't like me if I were powerful."

Or "Power is something that people with money or fame or status have. I don't have those things."

Or "I don't like to think of myself as powerful. Powerful people are bossy and manipulative. They run over you and don't care about you. I'm not like that."

Yes, we are ambivalent about—if not outright turned off by—the thought of claiming power. And for good reason. We look out into the world for examples of power, and we don't like what we see.

I understand. It took me many years before I began to claim and even celebrate my personal power. As a young girl growing up in the South—with red hair, no less—well, let's just say I was either praised for my leadership, my outgoing nature, and my intelligence or I was vilified. I was either the teacher's pet or ridiculed for being too bossy, too loud, or too much. So I got the message that "shining your light" didn't always win you friends.

In my twenties I often landed jobs others wanted, and I was chosen for coveted positions. OK, that was nice. But then somewhere along the way, the tables would turn and I'd find myself being shunned by the very people who thought I was great yesterday. So the message here was, "Impress us, let us know you are a star, and then play small, fit in, and don't show us up."

Recently I was leading a workshop series about personal effectiveness, and we were looking at personal power. When the participants were talking about the dark side of their experiences with power, their biggest fears included being talked into doing something they didn't want to do by someone in a position of power and being fooled or duped or manipulated by power and looking foolish.

Clearly, we have our work cut out for us when it comes to claiming and standing in personal power.

How We Hide from Our Power

Yes, we do hide from our power. The reasons are varied, but there are some common themes.

We hide from our power because it can ask us to take a risk, go in a different direction from the crowd, or stand up and speak our truth with radical loving—radical because we don't have any idea what we will encounter and what reactions we will get when we express that loving. We risk losing or failing, striking out alone, or being embarrassed if others do not agree with us.

Simply stated, it's not safe.

Our human nature wants to fit in, stay comfortable, belong, and go along with the status quo. It doesn't like bucking the system or rocking the boat. And expressing power can cause quakes of anxiety that create cracks in the inner walls of our comfort zone.

So we hide. And one common way we do this is by pointing our finger at someone in a powerful position and saying, "See, I don't want to be like that," and running back to that safe place within. Or playing the Ms. Popular "I want to be liked" card—and selling out.

Even if you believe deeply that you don't have power, even if you avoid being in a position of power, even if you judge those who have power, you are still powerful. And you aren't fooling anyone but yourself.

Just because you are afraid that someone won't like you if you are powerful, you still have power.

Even if you believe you have to have money, fame, or status to be powerful, and you don't have any of those, you are still powerful.

And if you see powerful people as bossy or manipulative, guess what? You are still powerful.

Power is energy—a presence, a strength, a conviction,
and a sovereignty over your life.

The dictionary defines "power" as the "ability to do something or act in a particular way, especially as a faculty or quality, e.g., the power of speech."

If you have ever created anything—from a nice meal to a work of art—or birthed a child, or created a relationship, a family, or a business, you have wielded personal power and ambition to do that. Creation is powerful. And when you begin to see your power and ambition harnessed in service to that sacred vision you hold in your heart, you realize that they can be employed in service of creation as well.

Here is a second dictionary definition for power, which is probably what leaves a bad taste in your mouth: "the capacity or ability to direct or influence the behavior of others or the course of events, e.g., the idea that men should have power over women."

All of us have had times in our lives when we felt powerless, or that someone or something else was holding the power. When that happens, the balance of power does not feel equal. Mistakenly, however, we believe that if they have power, we don't. So power is experienced as the winning hand; only one person or group can have it at a time.

That may be the moment you decide to strive for the symbols of power so the icky feeling doesn't surface again. But even if you acquire these outer trappings of power for yourself—money, position, fame, a big house, etc.—you will discover that they don't create a true and lasting experience of power.

Power symbols are just that—symbols. They cannot substitute for the real thing.

As long as you keep looking "out there" to decide whether or not you are powerful, you will come up short. The key is to redefine the experience of power for yourself and begin to see the personal power—and even the true power—in who you are.

New Reflections of Your Power

I want to help you have a new relationship to power and, through that relationship, begin to claim and celebrate the powerful creator you are. Redefining power for yourself can liberate you from eons of self-oppression and family

oppression. The world needs examples of new manifesta-
tions of power, and unless we walk the walk and embody
that authentic power, humanity will not have a role model
for it.

So I offer below two concepts for you to consider and
begin to see how power can be redefined and, therefore,
reclaimed for you.

The Power of Your Presence

He sat with his grieving friend. She turned to him and said,
"Thank you for your presence. It's made all the difference."

One of the simplest ways you can be powerful is to be
present. There is nothing you need do when you are present
other than be yourself and bring all of yourself forward.
And it isn't just the other that will be touched. You will
feel the experience of presence. For many, this experience
can take us beyond our ordinary reality into what could be
called a transcendent moment. When fully present, you are
radiating your essence—that intangible but very real energy
that is unique to you. The knowledge—and acknowledge-
ment—of your own essence is a key ingredient of all sacred
callings. Like a secret sauce, essence is a personal flavor
that only you can express. But like the nose on your face,
it's hard for you to see. Being present in your essence—your
True Self—with someone creates an energy that is felt by
both of you. You are the divine witness. That experience is
powerful.

The Power of Your Loving

Loving is power, and your true power is loving. I remember the first time I ever experienced the rush of pure goose
bump, heart-expanded, unbridled loving. I knew my life

was about to change forever. It was not when I got married or when I gave birth to my children, although those experiences were indeed full of loving and joy. The moment was when I dropped all my defenses to a greater loving and felt every cell of my body start to vibrate with an energy that was in me but came from beyond me.

When you open up to the true loving of who you are, you tap into a reservoir that is endless and unlimited. I am not referring to personal love. Personal love is usually conditioned with expectations and preferences and can be turned off and on at will. "Yes, I love you right now because you did *abc*," or "No, I don't love you right now because you did *xyz*."

An experience of the truth of your loving is like finding home; you know it deep down in your bones. And it is the building block of all sacred callings and sacred ambition expressions in the world—your loving made manifest. To manifest it with presence, essence, ambition, and power, you must continually open up to this impersonal but astounding energy.

What if you began to know that each moment of your life was created by loving? Would this change how you hold the past? The future? This moment?

We have been seduced by the world into thinking that loving is dependent on another or requires that "perfect" happily-ever-after relationship to come along. I, like all girls growing up in this society, bought into this myth and spent many evenings waiting for and pining for my "prince" to find me. But I believe one of the bigger reasons this myth doesn't manifest—and we all know it doesn't—is so that we will go on a quest to find out if there is something more.

Does true loving really exist? Yes, it does. It exists in you as you, and is sourced beyond you. I refer to this experience of loving as living love. A sacred calling grows inside you by loving and removing the clutter that prevents you from experiencing it. Because sacred callings are for the greater good—not just your ego—they must contain the pureness of this living love, which is not corrupted by your will or controlled by your desires.

Sacred callings exist in the ether of that loving, which moves the earth around the sun, which breathes you and sustains your existence day in and day out. The process of opening yourself to this living love is, in my experience, a life-long exercise of peeling away everything that is not loving.

Allowing your sacred calling to live in you and through you will assist in this peeling-away process; you cannot fake a sacred calling. It vibrates you and lights you up in a way that is undeniable. And that energy is the power of your loving.

Reflecting on the power of your presence and the power of your loving, you may begin to realize that there are more ways to experience and define power than the world's superficial view of it.

I've made a list for your further consideration and con-templation. I consider each of the following to be another source of true power:

☀ The Power of Knowing Yourself

This power sources freedom. Truly free people are powerful. And when we know ourselves, we have less of the unknown to worry about and be sabo-taged by. You can count on yourself to show up.

☀ The Power of Trusting in Yourself

This power allows you to steady yourself when faced with a setback or disappointment. Trust is a rod of strength that you can count on to uphold your integrity, your expression of what is true for you, your commitment to not abandoning yourself when the going gets tough. Trust helps you to take the next step even when that step is wobbly or risky.

The Power of Celebrating Another

This power creates connection and expands your experience of success and abundance. This power is a generosity of spirit that overflows into all you create and everyone you meet. Generosity is contagious and dispels the myth that there is not enough to go around. Sacred ambitions thrive when you have an attitude of enoughness.

The Power of Openheartedness

This power charges each moment of your day with vitality and energy. You radiate light. Like enoughness, the light of openheartedness can bring clarity to inner confusion or self-doubt. Keeping your heart open clears the channels for inspiration and intuitive guidance to flow.

The Power of Stillness

This power creates space for your divine guidance to be heard. Following a sacred calling requires you to be still and quiet so that the energy of your calling can be embodied. Embodied callings flow outward into your life easily and effortlessly. They become your new normal—an inner foundation you can build upon with confidence.

The Power of Choice

This power puts the reins of your life squarely in your hands and sets you free from past blame and shame. When you acknowledge that you are responsible for all that you have created, you can choose to take care of what presents itself next without vilifying yourself or anyone else. Knowing you have a choice as to how you will respond is liberating.

The Power of Your Wild Creativity

This power allows you to walk off the beaten path and discover what is in the invisible realms waiting to be made manifest. Sacred ambitions require out-of-the-box thinking. Often a sacred vision has never been created before, and there is no established path for how exactly it will materialize into a particular form. Wild creativity comes from the divine ether.

The Power of Beauty

This power feeds the soul and brings joy—a power that keeps you inspired. Beauty is a way to draw from the well of your inner creativity and what you hold sacred. It can be simple, like noticing the sunlight dancing across the leaves of your favorite tree and allowing the power of that beauty to fill you.

The Power of Awe and Wonder

This power creates joy and delight, affording you another way to stay inspired. Awe and wonder also serve to connect you to your divine nature, which resides in the mystery of who you are and upholds all that is sacred within you.

The Power of Serving

This power expands your inner reference points so you know that your gifts and talents are making a profound difference on the planet. Sacred ambitions answer a need that all of us are hungering for at this time. Service is the highest form of loving, and serving from the power of your loving is a blessing for you and a blessing for all.

Now that you have redefined power for yourself, claim it. Declare it. And watch the universe respond.

Chapter Eight

Redefining Ambition

THERE ARE TWO RELIGIONS IN THE SOUTH: FOOTBALL AND beauty pageants. I entered my first beauty pageant when I was fifteen years old—the Miss Teenage Shreveport pageant, which was a feeder pageant for Miss Teenage America. And I won. No one was more surprised than me.

Growing up, I loved to sing and perform. That ambition showed up early in my young life. I tried out for every choir, every solo, every small drama production in my school, and I usually got the part.

But entering the beauty pageant—a suggestion from my parents—was a stretch. I would be competing against beautiful, talented girls from all over the city. What a setup! You are competing knowing that only one girl gets the crown. All the rest are losers.

So when I won and got the crown, I was shocked but secretly pleased that I was the winner, not a loser. That is how I used my ambition when I was young. I wanted to win. I wanted the crown or the trophy or the perfect score. Spelling bees, friendly foot races, cheerleader try-outs, essay writing, neighborhood games, auditions for roles in musicals—

all were about getting the prize and being seen as a winner. Losers, after all, didn't have what it takes.

My ambition was definitely fueled by a desire to feel a certain way about myself through receiving recognition and approval. As I got older, I realized that the world worked that way, too. The world celebrates winners, applauds those who take home the coveted trophy. And success goes to those who are the most ambitious. I grew up hearing over and over that "the early bird gets the worm" and other trite expressions encouraging victory.

Equating ambition with winning creates wounds around our ambition. Because, of course, we don't always win, do we? And sometimes when we don't win, we shame and blame ourselves or receive an unfavorable verdict from others.

My wound happened when I went out for yet another beauty queen title several years later and got second runner-up, which in my eyes meant I lost—big time. At that moment when I was standing on stage with the other "losers," I cut loose an inner tirade of self-shame and self-blame, damning the part of me that put myself in a situation where I could lose. I blamed myself for my foolishness. My pride was devastated. I swore I would never place myself in that position again. As I was standing on the stage under the bright lights, I shut down that ambitious part of me. And it would be years before I allowed her to express herself again.

When we hold ambition in a win-lose paradigm, like I did, the stakes are high. Rather than celebrate our innate ability to express our talents and gifts and appreciate ourselves for our courage, we turn on ourselves with much more vitriol than anyone else would ever deliver to us. "You are a loser and no good. You need to hide yourself away. I will not allow you to humiliate me again, so don't even think about longing to come out. The answer is no."

Ouch! No wonder as adults we are ambivalent about ambition.

What about our society's role models for ambition? On one hand, we admire ambitious people. They stand out, take risks, own the spotlight, and often show us greatness. But on the other, we don't fully trust them and we see clearly when they use their ambition as a put-down to others. Consequently, we sometimes use the word "ambitious" as a slur.

I often take a poll during my events to see who thinks ambition is admirable and who believes it is questionable or even bad. The latter always gets the most votes.

But ambition is inborn and pure in essence. To want to express our joy, our loving, our creativity, our energy, or our humor in the world is a wonderful gift. Ambition can show up in all kinds of ways when we are young. A desire to go out for the school sports team. A wish to excel in art class or to get into the choir. A drive to make good grades or be singled out for a certain ability or talent.

Putting ourselves out there does not guarantee we will be chosen for the team or get a part in the play or a seat in the choir. If all we are after is the approval of others or creating an image of being a winner, disaster is on the horizon. Inevitably the moment will come when we "lose," and how we handle that will make all the difference.

Unfortunately, we may shut our ambition down. We stop caring. We tell ourselves it doesn't really matter. And that innate gift of our uniqueness takes a back seat to staying safe, hiding out, going along to fit in.

Ambition becomes way too risky.

We abandon a dream to become an actor; we give up our tuba lessons; we stop playing baseball or quit the swim team; we don't try out for cheerleader because the last time we tried we weren't chosen; we stop sharing our latest inventions because the professor thought they were too weird; we mess up on purpose because our efforts weren't perfect enough for our family the last time.

We abandon our potential greatness.

Sacred ambitions awaken these painful memories—and also the deep longing to come out of hiding. Your greatness resides in your sacred calling and in having the courage to heal the old wounds.

We need sacred ambitions to bring our greatness into the world.

Can Your Ambition Be Sacred?

It is a common belief that if you are ambitious you are consumed with "me, me, me" all the time. Most of us reject that view of ourselves. But what if that inner compelling drive to share who you are and your gifts and blessings in a much bigger way is sacred? What if that part of you that is so ready to stop hiding—the part that yearns to live a more authentic and heart-focused life—could be a blessing for you and for others? And what if that deep desire you have to be of service to other people and make a difference in their lives could also be served by your ambition?

Lenka's Story: From Doing to Being

"I did not know what sacred ambition was when I first joined the Sacred Ambition event [in] 2014. I also did not know how significant the experience would be to my life," Lenka told me.

"In 2014 I had been seventeen years in business—goal-oriented, organized, driven—and here I was attending a retreat focused on sacred ambition. I was traveling from Prague to Albuquerque, New

Mexico, not knowing anyone except Rebecca. This was a huge leap of faith."

Recalled Lenka, "Since that retreat, everything has changed. I am grateful that I came to the event not knowing what to expect. After the event I had my doubts. I was not sure how to implement what I had learned, and I struggled to see how the spiritual work could be implemented into my business world. I thought one does not support another. I was mistaken. I had to heal the parts of me that were hurting.

"In my career at that time, my ambition was driven by the external world without me realizing it. When it got hard, I worked harder. I had to overcome challenges, failures, falls, but I always got up and started again. I did not know how much I was hurting inside, I did not listen, and ignored my inner voice," she continued.

"I realized that I was scared and resisted my life, my power, gifts, and voice. I was hiding behind the work and the corporate world for fear of judgment, shame, and rejection. I also resisted the 'unknown.' Up until the teachings of sacred calling and sacred ambition, all I knew was 'doing,' achieving and delivering the aimed results. And I did not know how to create balance and connection between the business self and my spiritual self."

Lenka found that her new awareness and intentions shifted. While before she had been driven by action and accomplishment, she began to discover the balance and peace that is always present inside her.

"My sacred calling is courageous love beyond borders, and I am in the process of discovering how it wants to be expressed in the world," she said.

"The big 'aha' moments are doing versus being and actually doing from my being. I am learning to love, appreciate, and celebrate myself unconditionally without a 'corporate' brand. I am learning to surrender, to accept, forgive, and let go of all that does not serve me."

Lenka went on: "It feels like jumping off the cliff, but with the difference of knowing that I have the tools—and massive support from Rebecca and my sacred ambition tribe. I wanted to measure my spiritual progress like I used to measure my 'doing.' I am learning that progress is measured through my levels of awareness, inner peace, and energy. It makes me very humble to see how different my life is now compared to where I was in 2014. I am still an ambitious woman, but the ambition comes from within (more than ever), rather than the external world. Achieving great results does not have to be a fight or hard work. I work a lot on my self-awareness, compassion, trust, and connection to my inner self."

I asked Lenka if she felt her ambition was sacred.

"It is, I believe. And it is much bigger than I can comprehend. I am learning more and more to trust myself and the process. My understanding of 'sacred' is that I came to this world this lifetime to serve my unique purpose, and it is divinely guided."

Your ambition comes from a deep honoring of who you are. And when your ambition is employed in service of what you are devoted to, what you are committed to, or what lights up your heart, that ambition is sacred.

Do you care deeply for others and want them to live a fulfilling life? Does the face of a hungry child galvanize a conviction inside you to do something about it? Do you love to share your knowledge about health and nutrition so people can heal themselves? Do you want to change the culture of business in your field of expertise so the common good is served?

All these worldly needs require you to bring your ambition to the forefront if you want things to change. Your blessing, your knowledge, your heart, your new ideas will not be effective if no one knows about them and no one knows you. It takes ambition to open your mouth, raise your hand, offer help, share your expertise, make a phone call. And when your ambition serves your deepest devotion and your heart's commitment to be of service, that ambition is sacred.

Sacred ambition is a blessing to you and to those you serve. Sacred ambition is not so much about what you do as it is about bringing your True Self into what you do.

In the end, what you do for others—the offering you create, the business you launch, the lives you touch—ultimately awakens you more to who you truly are. And who you truly are is the blessing.

CHAPTER NINE

Facing the Inner Demons with Compassion

THROUGHOUT THIS BOOK I HAVE MENTIONED that the decision to answer the inner call with a "yes" and manifest it as a sacred ambition expression in the world will be fraught with challenges. The outer challenges can be formidable: low or no cash flow, failed launches, rejection, lack of avenues to be seen and heard, offering something no one seems to need or want, and not finding your tribe of like-hearted

Starting something new is always met with a fair amount of "Oops! That didn't work out!" moments. But by far the greatest obstacles to staying the course and getting up one more time than you are knocked down are the inner demons that plague all dedicated and devoted sacred calling pilgrims.

What are the inner demons? And how do you face these intruders that seem to want to vanquish your heart's calling? Let's start with the three biggies.

INNER DEMON #1: Fear

The list of fears that appear as you step onto the path of manifestation is endless: fear of being seen, fear of sharing what is precious with a callous world, fear of failing or looking like a fool, fear of your power, fear that you are an imposter, fear of not being enough.

INNER DEMON #2: Self-doubt

The world will test your resolve by putting in your path naysayers whose unkind words or dismissive expressions can cause you to stumble and reexamine (for the umpteenth time) whether your calling is legitimate. The self-doubts can include doubting who you are and the validity of your ambition; doubting whether you have the right or the qualifications to step out and make a difference; doubting your voice, your creative expression, and your ability to say what is in your heart that needs to be said; and doubting yourself to do what it takes to stay in the ring and not throw in the towel.

INNER DEMON #3: Self-Blame and Self-Shame

Your self-talk when you encounter your first setback can be cruel and damning. If self-doubt causes us to stumble, self-blaming can bring us to our knees. Assumptions and expectations are the bedmates of self-blame. You have an expectation around the number of clients in your practice, the number of sales, the feedback from the course or workshop, the positive response from an important meeting—and those expectations are not met, not by a long shot. First comes the tirade of blaming thoughts about what you did or did not do correctly, and then, fairly quickly, the shaming thoughts finish you off.

When do these inner demons present themselves? They could show up soon after you have that first instinctual, ambitious push from the inside to get something out there. You talk to friends, write a blog, post on social media, craft a story, paint a painting, design a business card, or rent an office or storefront—and then the first wave of "Wait a minute, what have I done?" hits you, and the undertow of voices speak up loud and clear: "What will people think?" "Who am I to speak out like this, anyway?" "I'm not original."

Or perhaps you have been honing your calling for many years and envisioning how that might look in the world, when an opportunity finally presents itself. But there is a backpedaling, a hesitation that you feel immediately. Your self-doubt speaks up: "Well, I really need to take one more class or course." "I don't think I'm really ready. It's too soon." "I'm not sure if the timing is right." Subtle? You bet. But just as effective at derailing any forward momentum.

Now you might be wondering why these voices are so loud and persistent. After all, if your sacred calling is to serve the greater good and make a change for the better, why is the universe not supporting you?

Because in order to live your sacred calling and create your sacred ambition business or social initiative, you have to get bigger.

To get bigger, to expand all the qualities needed to manifest your sacred ambition, you must embody and radiate your loving and power more fully and be willing to be seen without the masks or superficial glamour of your ego-personality. And to do this, you have to confront what gets in the way—all the fear, self-doubt, self-blame, and self-shame that hold you back. So you will be challenged. How you meet those challenges will make all the difference.

How to Expand Your Heart Radiance and Loving

Carrying a calling and embodying the energy that is compelling you to bring forth that calling requires you to go to school on yourself. If you approach a calling with fear and self-doubt or spend time shaming and blaming yourself, you will not get far in your quest. To put it bluntly, *you will give up*. And understandably so. That road is way too hard to travel.

The alternative is to learn new inner skills to recognize and work with those habitual knee-jerk mental and emotional reactions so you can create new pathways of choice—choices based in self-loving and self-compassion.

A self-loving approach begins with telling yourself the truth. Why is this hard for most of us? Because the ego-personality would rather maintain the status quo of avoidance and denial rather than confront the inner negative self-talk that is running amok. The fear of examining this self-talk is often a fear of revealing deeply hidden inner pain.

Truth-telling and living a sacred calling are wedded.

The opposite of negative self-talk is not positive self-talk. Instead it is a loving and compassionate shift, from seeing a narrow version of yourself through the eyes of lack to seeing all of you with the eyes of abundance—the abundance that comes from knowing your True Self and the loving that you are.

When sacred callings are being stirred awake, unconscious triggers from our past—of not-enoughness, of a belief about failing, of a fear of not doing it right—can swamp us unexpectedly. Someone makes a remark that is just a bit unkind and suddenly you are inundated by a tsunami of self-reproach.

On the journey of self-awakening, a sacred calling requires us to examine the unconscious beliefs about telling ourselves the truth, so we can champion the discovery and revelation of that inner truth.

Getting those feelings out into the open, speaking them out loud, frees up your energy. Your whole body can relax. And when you tell yourself the truth, you can decide if you want to take a deeper look to discover if there are patterns or limiting beliefs or debilitating fears running underneath.

This experience of telling yourself the truth can feel like being struck by lightning—in a good way. When truth is revealed, the entire energetic body registers the experience as a trembling or a shot of electricity or a whoosh of energy that wakes something up inside, something you didn't even know was there.

Before I began speaking truth to myself, my typical response to the question "Rebecca, are you OK?" was "I'm fine." If I was feeling anger or disappointment and was asked if there was something going on with me, I would reply, "Oh, no, nothing."

I had been taught and conditioned not to tell the truth about my feelings. What was modeled in my family was to keep all the "bad" and "ugly" feelings hidden and only show the "happy" or "nice" ones to the world.

When I began to speak the truth out loud about what I was feeling or how I was berating myself, I couldn't do it without trembling, and oftentimes without a lot of tears. This skill was so new to me that I also felt unmoored and lost in an experience that would completely overwhelm me. My body would register so much energetic shifting, shaking, and releasing that I was exhausted after allowing myself to express my feelings.

While this was happening, I could feel the cells of my body coming awake. I was vibrating at a different level. I walked around not feeling the same in my body. My face changed shape. I took up residence in my skin for the first time. And I looked more present and more real.

Feelings are energetic gateways you can pass through to arrive at a greater place of who you are. Habitual negative self-talk can point to an unresolved memory that suppresses the valuable gift of your aliveness and unique expression.

This greater place of who you are—where your unique expression and essence lives—fuels the conception of your sacred calling and builds the foundation on which you will erect your sacred ambition expression. But until you learn how to transmute all your inner baggage through self-loving, the sacredness of who you are cannot take up residence and thrive.

Kathleen's Story: The Human Side of My Sacredness

"My sacred calling is to know the essence of who I am, to embrace myself as the being that I am with my challenges and my gifts and my loving. As I bring forward my loving and self-acceptance for myself—this is really important to me—how can I bring the genuineness of that loving to the work I do?"

This was Kathleen's prayer.

Kathleen's upbringing was the antithesis of compassion and acceptance. She grew up in a judgmental shame-based home and religion and, consequently, as an adult, treated herself the same way, with lots of self-loathing.

She also had assumptions about what spirituality, self-compassion, and self-loving really were. "I realize now after years of doing this work that it's not about sitting in a lotus position and chanting, but about being really authentic," she said.

She has devoted many years to learning how to replace self-blame and self-shame with self-acceptance, self-compassion, and self-forgiveness. And her life has shifted. Kathleen's career, which involves being an advocate for children and their families, constantly challenged her to bring her compassion forward in situations that could be contentious and even litigious.

"Today there was an experience where I had to prepare for this court appearance," she recalled. "So I asked myself: 'How will I speak the truth without being so judgmental?' I don't want to be so activated to prove my point that I don't maintain my compassion at the same time."

Her example of applying self-loving to a potentially triggering situation shows the power of inner self-mastery on the front lines of life. The ability to move from a human-nature reaction and access compassion beyond our habitual responses demonstrates an inner mastery that grows within when we learn to let go of past unconscious limiting beliefs and judgments.

In Kathleen's court appearance she focused on letting go of control, surrendering to the highest good, staying centered in who she was, and aligning her ambition and power to her sacred commitment to herself. This was a masterful choice.

"Being aware of my own judgments of myself and how I judge others has taught me what self-compassion really is," she said. "Comparing myself to others and saying inside 'I'm not enough' has been a big challenge for me in my professional life. So the inner journey of self-mastery and the spiritual work has been so important. I can be my worst critic. But the more I can show up for myself and use the self-mastery tools, the more I can shift."

How has this new, deeper experience of self-compassion enhanced Kathleen's work in the world?

Well, for one thing she no longer looks outside herself to blame her coworkers or her circumstances or her boss for her misery. Several years ago Kathleen was in a job she knew she had to leave. So she opened her own practice, and guess what? All the things that bugged her about her last job she now was experiencing just with herself. Hmmm ... This was an eye-opener for Kathleen.

She began to see her old habits—extreme busyness, avoidance, and constant distractions from self-care and her spiritual life—as ways of not loving herself.

"So I went into the deeper work and looked at myself, what I create, and the choices I make, and realized I really don't have balance. I'm re-creating all the misery just with myself. This was humbling. I discovered a deeper level of waking up to how I can show up in a deeper way for myself. This is a new level of self-compassion for me."

Currently Kathleen is looking at the whole area of self-care and self-compassion with new eyes, resulting in her "making time for my spiritual practice, making time to exercise, making time to be with friends and family, making time to do my inner work and surround myself with people who support that." This was balance for Kathleen.

Being able to balance care for ourselves with care for others involves following inner guidance and asking, "Is this a compassionate choice for me?" rather than always answering to the chorus of "shoulds" from the ego-personality.

"Putting myself last is not self-loving, self-nurtur-
ing, or being compassionate with myself," Kathleen
said. "Taking care of myself first is not selfish, as I
was raised to believe. When I take care of me, I show
up in the abundance of who I am. This is greatest gift
I can give to others."

Loving Yourself Awake

My ninth-grade civics teacher was scary. His reputation in
the junior high was well-established before I took his class.
And this class was required for passing ninth grade.

He was not intimidating in stature. But the energy he
carried was huge. He would walk into class just as the final
bell was ringing, stand in front of the room, and call our
names, one by one, in a commanding voice. Our response
had to be, "Here, sir." Nothing else. And if for some reason you were distracted or responded in another way—like
simply saying "yes"—he would give you a look that sent
cold shivers up and down your spine.

I was repulsed and at the same time fascinated by him.
He commanded respect. But he also gave it. And when he
began teaching, he made the U.S. Constitution and the Bill
of Rights come alive. He taught civics in such a way that we
couldn't help but become better people.

As the year progressed, I came to adore his class. His
huge energy and presence never changed, but instead of
perceiving these things as intimidating, I came to know
them as loving. Yes, my ninth-grade civics teacher had a
huge heart. He loved teaching. And he loved us.

But it wasn't the kind of love that offered a soft place
to land. Instead, his love asked us to step up, to wake up,
to respect ourselves more, and to stop playing our childish
games. He was very clear about what he expected of us,

and when we matched his expectation and rose to the occasion, he beamed. And I knew I had not just made a good grade, I had matured in a new way. And it felt great.

Building a sacred ambition business or championing a sacred calling social initiative will require that you step up to greater maturity. Learning the tools to begin to love and respect yourself, keep your commitments, work with fear in a new way, dance with uncertainty and the unknown—and sacrifice your "old story" and the need to be liked—will save you from giving up and dashing your brilliance into a pit of despair.

Claiming a sacred calling and bringing it out in the world demands inner work.

When you apply and practice inner tools that remove unconscious beliefs and limitations, your energy shifts. You see with new eyes—eyes that view the world and your life through the lens of loving and compassion—and you no longer fear the journey. Instead you trust yourself and your divine power as you begin to see all of your life as for you, not against you.

What is rooted in the sacredness of your life—that treasure trove of blessings, unlimited possibilities, joy, happiness, grace, and what I call your "inner heaven"—can shine. The radiance of this heaven is what will light your way, step by step, and reveal to you aspects of yourself that you would not have discovered had you not opened up to the greatness of who you are.

PART THREE

Sacred Action

Take steps in the world that are aligned
with your calling and with manifesting
your sacred ambition. They will be
fueled by your radical loving.

Chapter Ten

Sacred Action Is Radical Loving

At some point in the emergence of your sacred calling, while you are facing the inner demons and doing the inner work necessary to support yourself, you must move into action. Like ships, sacred callings that evolve into sacred ambitions are not designed to stay safely tethered in the harbor. You must untie yourself from the comforting dock of your journaling and visioning and waiting and procrastinating and studying and sharing with only a few close friends—and set sail. There is a time when your sacred calling answers the crying need of the world, and the world is ready.

That step, however unsteady and uncertain, is an act of radical loving. It is radical because you don't have any idea what reactions you will encounter: praise or indifference, acceptance or rejection, understanding or confusion.

Regardless, every encounter will be a teaching, a learning, an opportunity to build inner strength and inner resolve and to clear away a bit more of those pesky self-sabotaging beliefs. When you launch your sacred calling, you sail into the storm, not away from it. And that's why you need to keep your heart's desire blazing and your eyes peeled—so you can stay the course and withstand the occasional monstrous wave. Clear, bold, and fierce loving fuels your heart and is necessary for engaging in radical loving action. When you take a step, however small, that's sustained by your heart-fire, sacredness appears in your action and is met by the unseen forces of the benevolent universe. Then a blessing is brought forward and you know you are on the right track.

Sacred callings take us into the territory of the heart, which can be experienced as vulnerable, messy, and raw. Our job is not to run from the rawness but to transmute it into an energy that can reach and impact those who have eyes to see and ears to hear, those that you have been called to serve.

I received this email from a student in my Sacred Ambition Mentorship program who shares her experience of radical loving and her choice to move into sacred action:

"I'm becoming an activist about climate change. It is real, it's happening, and I want the polar bears to have a chance to survive the melting of the arctic ice due to the heating up of the atmosphere. When I lived in Alaska and watched all the development, my heart was in great pain. I chose to look at how to heal my heart, not realizing the enormity of that project. I am now able to open my heart, to feel the pain of the world around me and begin to stand up and take action on behalf of the animals and environments I love."

This is a bold declaration of radical loving, because she did not allow the pain to shut her down or break her heart. She chose to let the pain and the love move her into action.

Radical loving—transformational, far-reaching, and impactful—first touches us so deeply that sometimes we can barely breathe or speak. But as we move the energy from inner awareness to outer action, it begins to support forward momentum and sustain our persistence.

Sacred ambitions need radical loving.

Many days you will feel all alone beating the drum of your sacred cause. Your ability to tap into the depth of your loving will propel you to take one more step, make one more call, write one more word, to paint, dance, speak, and share one more time.

How Radical Loving and Sacred Action Go Hand in Hand

Radical loving requires us to keep our heart open. And many times, it feels too painful to do that. When we are coming from radical loving, we are all-in—doing what we can with what we have, even if there is outrage, even if we feel helpless and hopeless, even in the face of others' worldviews that would diminish us. It is radical not to allow the despair or outrage in society to take us into a place of helplessness or hopelessness. Radical loving empowers each of us to take steps, small or large, toward *what we want,* not toward denouncing what we don't want.

Radical loving requires you to be real about the price you will pay. When your heart is ripped apart by what you have to confront within, you realize there is a price inherent in the question, "What expression of your radical loving will you bring to the world now?" You may see that the price entails sacrificing a need to protect yourself from what you perceive will overwhelm or destroy you. It is in those moments that you must let go and surrender to what your radical loving would have you do. So you face the overwhelm and do the inner work necessary to expand your heart beyond the capacity you believe it can handle.

When your heart is not free of past heavy baggage, you can't hold the painful weight and the loving at the same time. A resilient heart is free and expanded, so it has the space to hold both the pain and loving simultaneously.

How do we allow the heart to grow in depth and resilience? By clearing and healing what imprisons us. This creates space to be with the pain and at the same time move forward from a greater place of compassion.

Compassion is loving in action and a main component of radical loving. Compassion takes the fire in our heart and puts it into our hands—hands that can touch, heal, create, comfort, and bring into form something new. Compassion sees all and does not turn away from the ugliness of cruelty or hate. Rather than strike out and create more rancor, compassion moves in the direction of justice grounded in sacred action, in service to the greater good.

Radical loving requires sacred action. Our bond with the sacred is not in righteousness but in the alignment of each action with wisdom, loving, and what each of us holds as holy and blessed. We must be responsible with the fire in our hearts and constantly bring our projections of wrongdoing back to ourselves for inner reflection, acceptance, and forgiveness.

The fire of sacred action ignites inspiration, liberation, and freedom. In the presence of hate, it promotes loving; in the face of lies, truth; in the energy of fear, courage; and in the depth of darkness, light. Radical loving affects the fundamental nature of the underlying causes of what is not loving and creates far-reaching and thorough change.

Joanna's Radical Loving: To Be All Used Up

Joanna expressed her sacred calling in this way: "I feel and I know I am doing the soul work that I came here to do: serving the expansion of consciousness and awareness on the planet." But it took her many years, fifty-nine to be exact, to claim her sacred calling and move into sacred action.

Joanna said she had to live her life first, and, she quickly added, "I had to learn to love myself first."

Loving herself no matter what was the impetus that allowed her radical loving to manifest into a sacred ambition form.

"I've had an insatiable need to ask questions since I was a child," Joanna continued. "My life has a life of its own, which took me on a path that created increasing longing and inquisitiveness. So when I learned to love myself sufficiently, I could see outside myself that I wanted to ask questions of people who I believed had wisdom to share about consciousness and our place in the cosmos."Her radical loving took the form of a weekly radio show.

"My sacred calling is really about being useful or used up. I love the idea of being used up by the time I die." This is a radical loving statement.

I asked Joanna to explain more about what she meant.

"My life asks me, in order to breathe, to love myself fiercely no matter what shitty thing I've done. My life asks me to be real, and if I'm not real

I know it—and when I know that I feel shame. And I think that shame is the opposite of life. I don't want to feel shame. I want to feel the innate dignity that is my birthright."

Joanna continued: "Dignity, to me, is connecting in an essential way to what is alive and gives me more life force. And what is the life force for? This life force is given to me so I can connect more and more and more, and be in the community of living beings that make up the cosmos. If I follow the path of courage and dignity, which is not always easy, I get instructions as to what to do. It's a recursive process. It comes in and goes out in relationship to all living things. It's life-giving, life-sustaining, from courage and dignity. Sharing my life force through writing, speaking, and engaged conversations is to be in service to what created me. And when I die, I hope all of that life force will be used up."

Note: Joanna got her wish. She departed the earth before this book was published, leaving behind a circle of adoring fans and intimate friends and family who will carry forward the loving she demonstrated. Her life force was all used up. Thank you, Joanna. We are grateful for what you poured into each of us.

Chapter Eleven

Making Your Sacred Ambition Real

The invitation now is to make your sacred ambition expression real. If you want it to support you financially, you must do what it takes to grow your business. If your business needs to morph, you must create a transition strategy and implement the necessary changes.

If your sacred ambition is a creative project, such as completing that manuscript, hanging your first visual arts show, finishing the song you are writing, or picking up that instrument after so many years, what do you need to make that happen?

Social causes usually involve a tribe of people who are already passionate about the same thing and would love to come on board with your project. Reaching out, going to meetups, posting on various social media platforms—all are ways to gain momentum and find those who resonate with your calling.

Stay in touch with your inner process. If you find yourself slipping into negativity, comparisons, backpedaling, fear, or self-doubt, check in with a trusted mentor or a supportive group moving in the same direction. Ask yourself this question and be honest with yourself in answering it: "Are these doubts telling me I need to go inside and incubate some more, or are they masking the next layer of limitations that I need to clear?"

Often, the momentary hesitation is the next layer that is surfacing so it can be loved, accepted, and turned into sacred action. The invitation, as I see it, is to step out and take that precious expression into the mainstream. It is time to legitimize your offerings and bring them to Main Street.

Sacred ambition businesses, social causes, and creative projects can no longer be sidelined as countercultural, feel-good, "kumbaya" expressions. Sacred callings are emerging at this time because the world is craving an increasing population of people with new eyes to see—and new ears to hear—the new avenues available for attaining freedom, peace, equality, happiness, fulfillment, and inner riches. And we want the health of our society and businesses to reflect the health of our hearts and souls.

Calibrating our success by a yardstick that measures an abundance of money is no longer the ticket to freedom. This is a trap—yes, a bright, shiny trap but a trap nonetheless—that can snare you in the belief that at the end of a long week of fifteen-hour workdays, missed kids' recitals, and compromised health, happiness is waiting for you. It's a lie and an illusion.

You cannot manifest sacred ambitions in the midst of chaos, high emotions, urgent deadlines, or cash-flow crises. Quite honestly, the sacred is just not on those frequencies. Learning the keys and practicing the skills to manifest your dream in spirit-led timing, in service to the greater good (not the ego-personality), is part of what is being asked of you at this time. There's one common question that comes forward soon after someone realizes the fervor in their heart and recognizes the work they are called to do: "How will I make money in this?" Unfortunately, for many, it is a question that stops any further exploration. Yet what if it that question is exactly what will usher in all manner of unexpected possibilities? If the question is held as an opening rather than a dead end or roadblock, the way will continue to open up, revealing what is right for you.

Any service, business, or cause that meets a need will attract customers, clients, people of common vision, and markets to expand your reach.

The needs of our world are shifting rapidly. This is not your parents' world. It is your time to put your stake in the ground and stand in the vision of what you know.

What has precious value also has formidable challenges. Only you can decide whether the confrontation of those challenges will be part of the treasure you discover on your path of self-awakening and self-fulfillment.

Remember, sacred ambitions will ask everything of you. And when you give them your all, you will receive the abundant riches life has in store for you. Ask yourself: "How do I move forward with my heart's blazing ambition? How do I speak that deep, bell-ringing truth? What are the keys to manifesting that glorious vision or that barely audible but insistent whisper in my heart?"

Declaring your sacred calling is a crucial first step, but I have also identified seven steps for transforming sacred callings into viable businesses or social initiatives, so you can live the best version of yourself.

1. See the deeper truth of who you are. Journey back to yourself.

This step involves redefining power, reclaiming your innate ambition, and finding and welcoming home the parts of yourself that you have abandoned. Sacred callings require *all* of you to show up.

2. Redefine power and ambition and align it with your truth.

Just as power needs to be sourced from the deeper truth of who you are, so does your ability to express your calling to the world. Like power, ambition can serve your sacred calling and your business or social initiative when it is aligned with what is most sacred inside.

3. Remove the clutter.

Do the inner work to master the self-sabotaging voices; connect inside to your divine guidance; trust yourself; know your worthiness; and put the skills in place so you don't abandon your dream or get pulled off course.

4. Take a step. Begin.

Fulfillment is in the doing. The doing happens when our ambition meets the unseen forces of the universe. We don't know this energy until we take action. You spin your wheels and waste valuable life force when you sit around and think rather than begin.

5. Learn the tools and skills required to bring the essence of your sacred calling into form.

By creating practical plans for moving forward, you to allow the essence of your sacred calling the space and time to emerge. There is a dance of co-creation that begins when you set your plan into motion and are willing to let your calling lead you. Resiliency of the heart is required.

6. **Hold challenges, obstacles, and fear as signposts on the path, not as failures or signals for you to retreat.**

Expect fear to walk with you. Know that not everything you try will succeed. This is not an indication that you should admit defeat. It is simply part of the process.

7. **Increase your capacity to stay the course.**

Mature those parts of you that would rather stay in your comfort zone. Work with yourself in the face of disappointment and learn to course-correct. Find your tribe and a mentor. Don't go it alone.

The Story of Your Sacred Calling: Your New Testament for Our Times

Below are two stories of people who are living their sacred ambitions and following their sacred calling. These are not stories of emergence. These individuals, whose sacred ambitions serve the world, have been in business for many years or have completed a successful career and taken their gifts and talents into a greater service—for the greater good.

My intention in sharing these is so you can see yourself, dear reader. No story is perfect and no sacred calling is without its challenges. But my wish is that you will feel the deeper heart devotion and experience the blessings that these sacred ambition testaments bring to us all.

Deb's Story: One Dinner Table at a Time

I first met Deb when we were both members of a mastermind program. We had an immediate connection. We both sourced our deepest self when it came to what we wanted to do in the world.

Shortly after that, I hosted my first Your Sacred Ambition live event, and Deb attended.

She enrolled in the yearlong Sacred Ambition Mentorship to help her get clear about how she wanted to use her years of conflict-resolution skills now that she was officially retired from the corporate world. *And she wanted to show up as her True Self and bring her authentic voice and truth to her work.*

During the two years she was in the mentorship, Deb made an inner shift: Rather than approaching her work in the world from an old corporate model, she began instead to draw on her sacred ambition. But what really brought her current calling into focus was the political climate that prevailed in 2016. Deb felt deeply saddened by the rancor and division she witnessed between people of different races and colors. Her heart responded with a calling to take her years of experience in conflict resolution and use them to open up conversations between African American and white women.

Here is Deb's story, which exemplifies sacred calling, sacred action, and radical loving. For Deb, work that is sacred encompasses something bigger than just you or me. It involves other people and entails a holy element, which she refers to as "the greater good." It invites everyone it touches to be quiet and contemplative and to stay the course.

For the past three years Deb has been immersed in the work of discerning her own sacred ambition and sacred calling, which has led her on an inner journey to discover the blessing she wants to bring to the world.

"What does the world need, and what unique gifts do I have that I can bring to whatever issue

I am feeling called to?" Deb asked herself. She worked for many years in human resource departments of corporations. She considered her work to be important, but as she began to grow personally and gain more experience, Deb realized that being a voice for the management did not always align with her truth. The corporate work began to weigh on her heart. Once she retired and no longer had to make money, she was drawn to the sacred ambition that arose from the true calling of her heart. And she has been following it since.

"What surprised me was the direction of the conflict resolution approach that surfaced this year," she said. "I found myself wanting to do something about race relations—specifically the conflicts in race between African American women and white women ... and, at the same time, address the unconscious but oh-so-prevalent issues for white women of white privilege."

Deb grew up in Erie, Pennsylvania, and lives in the Chicago area, so she has seen and experienced firsthand the segregation, anger, prejudice, and suffering that the lack of dialogue between African Americans and whites has caused.

"We really do not know how to sit down with each other and talk openly," said Deb. And this, for her, was no longer tolerable.

So she reached out to an African American woman friend, who was also trained as a teacher of conflict resolution, and together they crafted a plan to form small groups of four to six women who sit around a table and talk openly about what is breaking their hearts in the political and sociopolitical environment. Part of Deb's dream is to foster compassionate listening so, as she put it, "we can heal the children and heal our communities."

One surprise she encountered was the response from her African American thought-leader friends when she asked them about white privilege. "Deb, we are tired of trying to bring white women along in understanding white privilege," they told her. "We think that is a conversation white women need to have with other white women—to raise their awareness and discover how owning their white privilege can help heal the rift in our communities."

"It seems to me," Deb recalled, "that in our current political climate, everyone has given themselves permission to voice their hatred of one ethnic group or another. I find that really disturbing." So she turned her heartache into sacred action.

Where is her sacred action today?

"Right now," Deb continued, "it's research and conversation time for me. I need to continue to ask questions and gather the responses so when our groups do start, we will have some sense of the territory and where to begin. This is soul work for me, and I realize that I need to go deep, have conversations, and proceed with a thoughtful research phase, rather than leap in with both feet. That's where I am, and it is really rich."

One of the inner treasures Deb has discovered in this sacred ambition social initiative is listening to her inner guidance and trusting herself more. She is centered on the truth and integrity of who she is—her True Self—and being her own person in the world. Showing up as herself is something she has had to grow into, but today it feels fabulous.

The seeds of this deeper calling were sown when Deb was very young. Growing up in her Chicago neighborhood, she was aware of sexual abuse, poverty, and strong emotions like anger. Deb's father helped instill in her that she and her family were to share who they were and what they had. This environment helped shape her worldview, and she realized that since her younger years in the 1950s and 1960s, not much has changed in those neighborhoods regarding race relations.

So she chose a conflict-resolution career in human resources specifically to assist people to learn to live more peacefully and agreeably with each other.

Deb's story illustrates the way sacred callings evolve over time. The seeds are often found in our early, impressionable years. Then later, they sprout and grow.

Where were the important learnings Deb received from her time in the Sacred Ambition Mentorship?

"Definitely knowing who you are is so important," she said. "Getting rid of a lot of baggage and things that just don't work anymore. Knowing that you are a divine being and that you have gifts that you can experience in much greater abundance when you are teamed up with others. And I would add that having an ongoing dialogue with your higher power, or whatever you call divine guidance, because that keeps you focused on the greater good so the inner fears do not get in your way."Deb's sacred ambition social initiative vision? Multiple groups of four to six women, all over Chicago, sitting around dinner tables or in someone's living room. She hopes that by securing grant money and other sources of support, she can facilitate the creation of these types of conversations—and they will spread throughout her city and beyond.

"But," Deb said, "we keep reminding ourselves that it's going to be one dinner table at a time."

Tanya's Story: My Sacred Ambition as Devotion

Tanya is a powerhouse when it comes to facilitating transformation through storytelling. She has been a mentor of mine, assisting me in bringing more of my heart and soul into the writing and stories I share. Tanya has been running a successful business as a storytelling coach for more than two decades. When I interviewed her, I wanted to start with the inception of her calling, because all sacred ambition businesses begin with those seminal moments.

Tanya's story started with tragedy. "When I was fourteen years old I went to my first acting class on the very day that my grandfather died. My mother said, 'Let's cancel your acting class.' Something inside of me said, 'No. Let me go.' And I was in terrible grief."

What transpired that day for Tanya was an epiphany. She was given a monologue to memorize by the acting teacher, and after about an hour she performed the monologue in front of the acting class.

"I memorized the piece. It wasn't hard for me," she said. "I got up on stage in front of the other classmates, and I went into an altered state. I did the monologue, and I had a shift in consciousness. I channeled all my grief and all my pain. And when it was over, I didn't understand what had happened. But I knew I was changed. I had taken all of my intense feelings and changed them through acting. In that moment, looking back, I understood on some level the transformational power of story and storytelling and theater."

The next turning point for Tanya was at age nineteen, when she attended a performance by storyteller Spalding Gray. In that performance he spoke about all the taboos that Tanya had experienced in her own family, and she realized she wasn't interested in playing roles in a traditional theater program. She wanted something more: intimacy.

"I knew I wanted to do what he did—express through storytelling and monologues how to live life. That was the night I realized my sacred calling. No matter that I didn't know how to write, I knew I had a code to crack. I woke up every single day for eleven years and said, 'I have to do a solo show.'" Tanya took writing classes and acting classes and developed a writing practice with one purpose in mind—to become comfortable enough to write a solo show. She wrote three shows that never got produced. She had no mentor; no one was teaching the work of solo monologue shows back then. But finally she wrote and performed her first solo show. Everything about her life fell into place.

When I asked Tanya to articulate her sacred calling, she said, "I am devoted to the art of stories through the medium of solo performance, memoir, conscious business storytelling ... To awaken, catalyze, and inspire myself and others. And my life works as long as I follow the path of story. If I get off the path of story, my life falls apart."

But it took several more years before Tanya was all-in. After performing her first solo show,

Tanya discovered she was unemployable. This knowledge was frightening and exhilarating at the same time. Suddenly she realized, "I have to make this work." Up until that time, she would indulge herself by looking for a "J.O.B." once a year. But as she went through each interview, her body reacted with a violent "no," and she knew that if she accepted the job, she would become ill.

So Tanya closed the back door. She took herself and her sacred calling seriously. And what happened? Her business revenue increased exponentially. She had no Plan B. She did not entertain doing anything but her sacred calling. I asked her if there were still challenges now, more than fourteen years later. "You never get over the 'what-ifs.' Every month I wonder if this will be my last client, my last show," she said. Even though she gets new clients weekly, Tanya has never been able to silence the voice of fear. "I am a person prone to worry and anxiety," she said. "I do my calling with panic and fear and money worries sitting on my shoulder." But she has also learned to manage those inner demons.

Does she believe her ambition is sacred?

"My ambition lines up with my internal mission. I know I am called by a higher power to do this work."

Tanya is clear that her storytelling and memoir facilitating has changed lives. And she knows she is a tool of the divine—that the healing and transformation that take place are not her doing. "But if I'm not willing to show up and do my part and arrange the workshop when I'm inspired and invite people in and ask the venue to donate the space ... If I'm unwilling to show up, then the divine doesn't have me to move through. And the blessing of that has kept me going."

Tanya went on to say that as a powerful woman in a patriarchal society, she was conditioned to be competitive with other women. But her wish is to be collaborative. "The more I've leaned into collaboration with my sacred ambition, the more successful and the happier I've become. I've created these amazing relationships with other powerful women who are peers."

Sacred ambitions are not designed to be top-of-the-pyramid, solo experiences. They are here for the collective, and it takes a collective to bring a sacred calling to the world. This is true for Tanya. "I get excited celebrating other powerful women. I'm honored to be a part of the collaborations. I say it this way: 'Your success is my success, and if we know they are linked, it is a game changer.'"

That is Tanya's definition of power—something relational and collaborative.

Does she face any other challenges? She immediately jumped into talking about the internet culture and marketing in today's world. We both agreed that the online offers of new strategies and "shiny objects"—ego hooks for having success and making a certain amount of money—do not work for sacred ambition businesses.

"Every day there is a question about whether I should do this marketing funnel or take this class with this person. It's so easy to get lost in the maze of bigger, better, shinier," Tanya said. "The challenge for me is to have the faith to step away from that. I am noticing I am going deeper into content marketing, which is me just being me. My marketing strategies are based on human connection: 'How do I bring in more income by being me? How do I get comfortable showing up to deliver this speech or monologue?' So realizing that, you may have an income cap that reflects the business model and serves in the way you want to serve. Knowing that and being honest about that helps you to not get hooked by the next shiny, new offer. The ego doesn't get distracted. You are following something greater, something that rings true to you on every level."Tanya's work extends far beyond the bounds of a career. "If I look at my work as my spiritual practice, as my devotion, first it infuses it with the sacred, and then it gives me the energy to keep going when I don't feel like it and when I am doing the hard part. So rather than it being a career, devotion is absolutely what fuels me. This is not a career path. This is my devotion. If this is your path and you can accept it, then all the gifts are really here."

CHAPTER TWELVE

Our New Testament

AT THIS TIME, OUR COLLECTIVE RADICAL LOVING IS asking us to write a new testament, a new story that will turn around the current train barreling toward environmental, economic, and cultural catastrophe. And not only to simply write a new story, but put it into action.

What do you want your world to look like twenty years from now? Do you want to see a more compassionate and kinder approach to the issues that challenge us as a human race? Would you like your environment to sustain all people with the basic necessities of healthy food, water, and air? Do you wish for an equitable standard of living so that all peoples can feel empowered and live their life in alignment with their values?

These are visions I would like to help make real over the next twenty years. And I believe my sacred calling will assist in that effort. What about you? Do you see your sacred calling serving the world you envision in twenty years?

I don't have a crystal ball or a magic wand. I know the times ahead will be fraught with chaos, upheaval, and push-back to the new change that is coming. I can almost guarantee you will have voices inside your head—and in your world— that disagree with the vision you are holding, as well as voices that will yell their approval. Neither voice is necessary to take into consideration when it comes to your heart's calling.

What is necessary is to ground yourself in the conviction of your sacred calling and keep your eyes focused on the good you were commissioned with when your soul took on a body this lifetime. You are not alone. There are millions of us waking up every day to the callings that have reverberated in our cells for decades.

Advancing the new story is going to require all of us envisioning, sharing, and talking about it with friends, in our spiritual and religious congregations, in our community, and with those who hold power to change policy. We need these new-story conversations to begin today.

The stories we have written up until now have served us in many ways and have gotten us to where we are today, for better or worse. However, there is a greater awareness of the places in our culture, our country, and the world that need our attention, our resources of time, energy, and sacred action.

We must not become overwhelmed with despair and resign ourselves to being passive observers of possible impending doom. We must choose to champion our hearts in service to the greater good. We must be seen and heard as we talk about, live, and share the new story. We must move toward what we want, not just rail against what we don't.

The seeds of this new story are germinating in your sacred calling and waiting for you to water them deeply with your energy, your commitment, your devotion, and your dedication. Sacred ambition businesses, social initiatives, and creative projects provide the rich soil where those seeds can sprout, grow in courage and resolve, and bear the deeply nourishing fruit that is life-sustaining and life-giving.

This book is my honest assessment of what it really takes to follow a calling. Sometimes we romanticize the work with lofty platitudes and inspired rallying cries. They have their place.

But the day-to-day work of deconstructing and reconstructing is a sobering labor of consistent devotion and dedication. It is as honorable now as it was any other time in our collective earth story when radical rebuilding and healing were needed. And the stakes are just as high.

My greatest wish, dear reader, is that you will take up your sword of truth and loving—not to do battle but to do good. I hope to see you out there.

Contributors

I know all the contributors in this book. They are bright souls who live their lives dedicated to a path of heart and bringing their highest calling forward. I extend my sincere gratitude to each one for sharing a bit of their story and blessing us with their blessing: a testament to the new vision and beauty that is emerging at this time.

Thank you to:

Kathleen Benecke
Sherry Campbell
Kim Carpenter
Deborah Kilgore Ford
Rikki Fowler
Joanna Harcourt Smith
Lenka Matthews
Bobbye Middendorf
Isabel Parlett
Laura Pedro
Tanya Taylor Rubenstein
Vincent St. Xavier
Mary Wakefield

Acknowledgments

This book was crafted and shaped by the depth and courage of so many beautiful souls who gifted me with the opportunity to give their sacred callings wings as they morphed into sacred ambition projects, social initiatives, careers, practices, and well-lived lives. I attribute the inspiration to write this book to them.

Manifest Your Sacred Ambition was first printed as a booklet and gifted to the attendees of the 2015 Your Sacred Ambition event. Now, after working on it in fits and starts over the last five years, I am finally giving it life as a full-fledged book. I feel she is now ready to stand on her own two feet and declare the bold reality of what it takes to birth a calling into form.

Great gratitude goes out to:

✦ The first person who spoke the words 'sacred ambition' to me and witnessed the profound recognition of my being to those words: Lissa Boles

✦ My early readers (with their helpful comments) Isabel Parlett, Reese Taylor, and Mary Neighbour

✦ My editors Jeff Braucher and Eve Tolpa

✦ My indie book strategist, Karen Bomm, who has shepherded me through several successful launches.

✦ My book and cover designer Diane Rigoli, who reads between the lines of my awkward words to fashion the perfect creation for my vision.

And, finally, I am eternally grateful to the Light that guides me and the Sound that is my ultimate calling ... calling me home.

REBECCA E. SKEELE is a Spiritual Mentor and Wisdom Teacher. An ordained minister, she holds two masters degrees: one in applied psychology and one in spiritual science. Previously, Rebecca published *You Can Make It Heaven: How to Enrich your Life with Abundance and Loving* (First and Second Edition) and the journal, *Keys to Make My Life a Heaven*. Her books are available through local bookstores and on Amazon. Rebecca leads workshops, retreats, and online classes in the U.S. and internationally. She lives in Santa Fe, New Mexico.

www.RebeccaESkeele.com

Resources

To Order:
Amazon Author Page:
www.amazon.com/author/rebeccaeskeele

Rebecca's website:
www.RebeccaESkeele.com/author

More information about the Heaven on Earth Wisdom
School and Rebecca's teachings:

Rebecca's Membership Site: Sacred Wisdom Teachings
www.RebeccaESkeele.com/membership

▶ Rebecca's YouTube Channel
www.YouTube.com/rebeccaskeele

Let's Connect!
f www.Facebook.com/rebecca.e.skeele
in www.LinkedIn.com/in/rebeccaeskeele
⊙ www.Instagram.com/rebeccaeskeele

Contact Rebecca:
www.RebeccaESkeele.com/contact

#1 NEW RELEASE ON
amazon

AVAILABLE ON
AMAZON AND
IN BOOKSTORES

Best Seller
amazon.com

2019 WINNER

You Can Make it Heaven
(paperback book)

Keys to Make My Life a Heaven
(paperback journal)

www.**RebeccaESkeele**.com

CPSIA information can be obtained
at www.ICGtesting.com
Printed in the USA
FSHW011755070222
88165FS

9 780971 567474